Georgian Tonbridge

The Editor
Dr Christopher Chalklin is the President of Tonbridge Historical Society and convenor of its Research Group, whose members are the authors of the essays in this volume. He was formerly Reader in History at the University of Reading, and has written widely on Kentish History.

Tonbridge Historical Society
The Society runs a regular annual programme which includes authoritative talks on varied aspects of local and general history, as well as visits to places of historical interest. Its Research Group has produced three books in addition to *Georgian Tonbridge*. They are: *Early Victorian Tonbridge* (1975), *Mid-Victorian Tonbridge* (1983), and *Late Victorian & Edwardian Tonbridge* (1988). All three were edited by C W Chalklin and published by Kent County Library, Maidstone. For details of the Society's current programme, and information on how to join, please contact the Hon. Sec., Tonbridge Historical Society, c/o Tonbridge Library, Avebury Avenue, Tonbridge, Kent TN9 1TG.

Cover illustration
'Tunbridge Castle', from an original by I Farington RA, 1795 (Source: Centre for Kentish Studies)

Georgian Tonbridge

edited by
C W Chalklin

Tonbridge Historical Society

The production of this book has been supported by a grant from the
Heritage Development Fund of Kent County Council

First published in 1994
by Tonbridge Historical Society
c/o Tonbridge Library, Avebury Avenue, Tonbridge, Kent TN9 1TG

ISBN 0 9523563 0 9

Cataloguing in Publication Data
A catalogue record for this book is available from the British Library

Typeset from Pagemaker 5 in 12 point Monotype Bembo
Cover designed by Addax Publishing, Tonbridge
Printed in England by Antony Rowe Ltd, Chippenham, Wiltshire

Contents

List of Maps and Illustrations   6

Acknowledgements   7

Foreword   9
Dr Joan Thirsk, CBE

Introduction   11
Dr C W Chalklin

The Landed and Propertied Classes of Georgian Tonbridge   23
Dr P L Humphries

Mabledon and its Owners 1803–1830   72
Gwenyth Hodge

The Work of the Town Wardens   83
Sydney Simmons

Education in Georgian Tonbridge   135
Dorothy Stammers

Tonbridge School 1714–1840   147
Sally Hedley-Jones

Five Properties on the Outskirts of Tonbridge 1740–1840   163
Margaret Stephens

List of Subscribers   198

List of Maps and Illustrations

Tonbridge Town and its vicinity in 1838 (map)   8

The Town Hall and upper High Street   14

William Francis Woodgate, 1770-1828   34

Mabledon, by Paul Amsinck   76

The first entry in the oldest surviving Town Wardens'   82
account book

Tonbridge and the surrounding area in 1799, showing   86
the Town Lands (map)

Extract from the Town Wardens' account book, 1759   101

The former Workhouse and Bank Street School   134

Tonbridge School as it was from 1760 to 1825   149

Stair Farm in 1748 (map)   166

Acknowledgements

The editor and authors would like to thank everyone who has helped with the preparation of papers for this book, and in particular the following: the staff of the Centre for Kentish Studies, Maidstone; the staff of Tonbridge Reference Library; the Skinners' Company; the Librarian of Tonbridge School, Jean Cook; Elsie Humphries and Eric Francis, who read in draft the essay on *The Landed and Propertied Classes;* David Davis and his fellow Town Wardens, who in 1987 made the Wardens' records available for study; Paul Baxter, the present Clerk to the Trustees of the Tonbridge Town Lands and Richard Mylls Charity, whose perspicacity and dedication saved their records for us; and especially the long-suffering wives, husbands and other family members who temporarily gave up their partners – and sometimes part of their homes – in the interests of historical research.

The Committee of Tonbridge Historical Society would like to express their gratitude to the authors of these essays, and to: Dr Joan Thirsk, for honouring us with a Foreword; Dr Christopher Chalklin, President of the Society, under whose guidance and leadership this book has been brought to fruition; Kent County Council, which has generously borne part of the cost of publication through the award of a grant from its Heritage Development Fund; Margaret Stephens, who read the entire text in proof; Natasha Machtus, Philippa Wilson and Alan Haley who helped with keyboarding and disk conversion; and Anthony Wilson, who brought a measure of unity to disparate contributions, typeset the book on his computer, and saw it through the press.

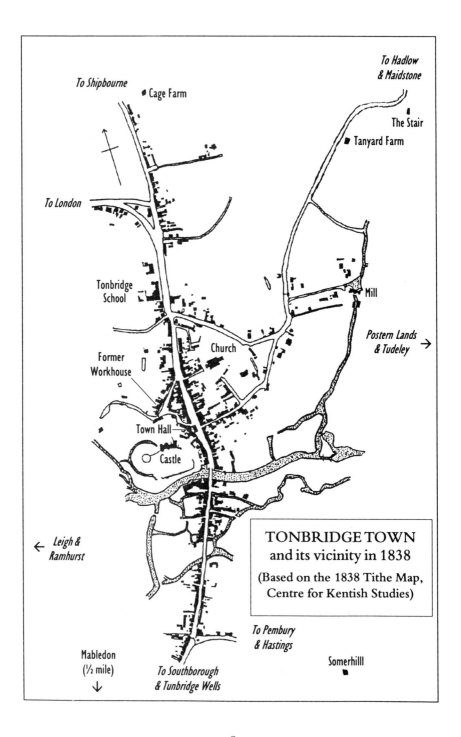

To Hadlow & Maidstone

To Shipbourne

Cage Farm

The Stair

Tanyard Farm

To London

Tonbridge School

Mill

Postern Lands & Tudeley →

Former Workhouse

Church

Town Hall

Castle

← Leigh & Ramhurst

TONBRIDGE TOWN
and its vicinity in 1838
(Based on the 1838 Tithe Map,
Centre for Kentish Studies)

To Pembury & Hastings

Mabledon
(½ mile)
↓

To Southborough
& Tunbridge Wells

Somerhilll

Foreword

Dr Joan Thirsk, CBE, FBA, Hon D Litt
Formerly Reader in Economic History at the University of Oxford

In the Georgian period, 1714-1830, Tonbridge embarked on a new phase of its life. From being an inconspicuous, unadventurous market town, it blossomed, improved its appearance, and attracted many more people to live in the area. This well researched account recalls that story, and will stimulate the imagination of all residents and visitors.

We need to be reminded just how large was the parish of Tonbridge in the eighteenth century, for it included both Hildenborough at one end and Tunbridge Wells at the other. The town was really only an island in a vast expanse of mostly pasture and woodland. But now its spa at the southern end of the parish began to attract permanent, instead of just seasonal, residents; much land in the parish, formerly consolidated in four great estates, came onto the market, and many more modest families were given the chance to acquire smaller parcels; the Medway became navigable as far as the High Street, whereas before it was navigable only to Maidstone. No wonder that the town, commercially and visually, entered on a new lease of life. It paved its roads, dried up all the muddy patches in the High Street, and repaired its bridges. The townspeople felt a fresh sense of pride, which prompted the building of a new town and market hall.

The story is vividly told here by local historians. They have studied innumerable documents of the period, and at every turn they link their findings with the town that we see today. They each bring different skills and interests to their task, but they are all intent on showing us the signs of the past that live on in the present. Thus they give a fourth dimension to our view both of the farms around the town and of the town itself, tracing the changes which turned one large parish into three smaller ones and earned for this modest timber-built town, with less than a thousand inhabitants in 1740, the far more alluring description of 1839, when its main street was 'remarkably clean', and it possessed 'a number of elegant and well furnished shops'.

As for the town's illustrious inhabitants, surely we must put first in the list, as does the *National and Commercial Directory* of 1839, Eliza Acton, living at Bordyke House, and already at work in its kitchen on her *Modern Cookery* (1845). It would make her the author of the most reliable and detailed recipe book that had ever appeared, valued today as 'the greatest cookery book in our language'. Elizabeth David has paid her full tribute: 'for twenty years the book has been my beloved companion – I have marvelled at the illuminating and decisive qualities of Miss Acton's recipes'. We can marvel too, for her book was reprinted in 1968 and later, but we can use it for yet another purpose. As local historians we can also catch a glimpse in Miss Acton's recipes of the varied groceries, fruits, and fresh fish – yes, fresh fish – then being sold in our Tonbridge shops.

Hadlow
August 1994

Introduction

Dr C W Chalklin

The ancient parish of Tonbridge was by far the largest in Kent with 15,378 acres. It measured some eight miles from north to south, and five and a half miles from east to west. Two or three miles from the northern boundary the River Medway crossed the parish from west to east, forming an alluvial belt varying from under half a mile to nearly a mile in width. It was meadow land. The district to the north-west (Hildenborough) is comparatively flat, with gentle slopes. This is heavy clay soil, difficult to work. The larger southern area (Southborough) is hilly with steep-sided valleys. Its sand, sandstone and clay is deficient in lime. Because of the soil, all except the low-lying riverside land had much pasture (particularly for cattle, and also sheep) and woodland in the mid-eighteenth century, with arable for oats, wheat, podware (beans, etc) and hops.

The small market town of Tonbridge of medieval origin with its castle and parish church was at the one river crossing. More than 150 wooden houses of one, two and three storeys lay beside the main street running from north to south. At the south end five bridges crossed the branches of the Medway. The high street was paved in the middle and had a few trees. Less attractive was the open drain from the shambles and livestock on market days. There were public and private wells, and pits for refuse in the yards and gardens.

The spa settlement of Tunbridge Wells which had emerged in the 1680s was partly in Tonbridge parish, on its southern boundary. There were no nucleated villages, only a hamlet beside Southborough Common halfway between Tonbridge and the Wells. Farmsteads and cottages, still of timber, were dispersed on the farms, comprising largely contiguous closes often bordered by copses with oaks and other timber. The holdings were relatively small. Twenty-three

11

tenants held 1,222 acres on the estate of Richard Children in Hildenborough and other parishes in 1743, an average of 53.1 acres per tenant. Fields were often small. The Town Lands comprised about 35 acres in nine closes. Landownership was also much divided.

The face of the town was transformed between the mid-eighteenth century and 1840. Bricks replaced timber as the main building material. This was because barges on the newly navigable Medway brought lime and chalk cheaply. Three big brick houses were erected by gentry between the 1730s and 1770s. In the High Street, shops, inns and dwellings were fronted or rebuilt fully in brick. In 1775 and 1814 the main bridges were reconstructed, and in 1798 a town and market hall was put up by the market owner William Woodgate, the biggest local landlord. The town was extended along the High Street and lanes leading off it with groups of cottages, terraced houses and the occasional villa. Paving was much increased and improved by the town wardens, as Sydney Simmons shows in his article on page 83. Drainage was a worsening problem especially among working-class tenements south of the river, where sewerage lay uncovered beside the High Street. Oil lighting was tried for several winters in the 1790s, but efficient permanent lighting did not come until the gas company was set up in 1836.

The rural landscape changed in detail only. Several mansions were built or rebuilt such as Mabledon which is the subject of Gwenyth Hodge's paper (page 72). Some farmhouses were re-erected in brick. Labourers' cottages had to be built, some on the edge of the town and in the rising village of Southborough, but mostly dispersed on the farmlands. Woods were cleared for agriculture in Southfrith. More soil was ploughed for wheat, oats and pulses, especially in the years of high corn prices between 1795 and 1813.

Before 1750 the population of the whole parish rose slowly, and was at least 2,000 by that date. It doubled by 1800 (Table 1.2). The advance was even quicker later, when the censuses give exact numbers. Thus in 40 years the inhabitants of the parish almost trebled, and by 1840 the population had grown six times since 1750.

This demographic transformation reflects largely the expansion

Introduction

of the two towns, and particularly the Wells. At least half the parish inhabitants were urban by the early eighteenth century. There were some 180 dwellings or about 800 people in Tonbridge town when its manor was surveyed in 1739. The Wells had several hundred inhabitants at this time. The former grew rapidly from the 1740s and 1750s. It may have had about 1,900 people by 1801, according to the proportion of parish ratepayers living in the town. In 1841 the manuscript census gives 3,115 inhabitants. The seasonal resort changed

Table 1.1: Number of Anglican Baptisms in Tonbridge Parish, by decade

1714-23   566   1744-53   676   1774-83   895   1796-1805   1,232

Table 1.2: Population in Tonbridge and some adjoining Parishes 1801-41

	Tonbridge	Leigh	Hadlow	Pembury	Tudeley
1801	4,371	739	1,115	742	417
1811	5,932	822	1,531	825	472
1821	7,406	876	1,757	891	546
1831	10,380	1,011	1,853	1,070	575
1841	12,530	1,245	2,108	1,093	643

slowly for most of the eighteenth century; then it became residential, and by 1841 6,053 of its inhabitants lived in Tonbridge parish. Southborough became a large village in the early nineteenth century, but the population of the rural parish remained sparse, largely on account of the remaining woodlands between Tonbridge town and Pembury. In 1841 there were about 140 people per square mile, compared with 166 in Leigh and 227 in Hadlow.

Several facts point to the modest prosperity of the parish and especially the town before 1740. In 1664 the town's population was 600; by 1739 it was about 800, as we have seen. In 1672 the weekly general market on Fridays was supplemented by a monthly livestock market, reflecting the importance locally of cattle farming. The town lay on Kent's second most important road, linking London with the Channel coast at Rye. It had a postmaster from 1672, and the route was used by carriers of fish for London. Because of the clay surfaces in the Weald, a section of this road through the town between Riverhill and Woodsgate with a branch to the Wells was one of the first to be turnpiked in England, in 1709. The use of the road from London to Tunbridge Wells grew during the period as the spa became more popular. However the effects of these changes in trade and transport compensated partly for the depressing influence on employment and wealth of the end of the local broadcloth industry.

Part of the more rapid growth of the town from about 1750 is explained by general demographic increase. The expansion of population in the neighbouring countryside as well as the town increased the demand on the services of the crafts and trades which were at the basis of the urban economy. No labour-intensive industries emerged, nor did Tonbridge develop as a residential centre for the well-to-do such as lesser gentry or retired tradespeople and professional men, although the schools were an undoubted attraction. Roads improved. In 1765 the route from the town eastward to Maidstone was turnpiked, and the road from Hildenborough to Cowden in the west. The route connecting the town to Ightham in the north was turnpiked in 1809. The parish lanes were being repaired out of highway rates at least from 1761. The main road between London and the coast was all turnpiked by 1762, and the routes from the Wells into Sussex by 1767. The turnpike trustees collected tolls and raised loans to widen and improve the foundations and surfaces with stone. At least from the 1800s to 1836 gradients were lowered and new cuttings made. Road carriage of lighter goods and people rose sharply. In 1803 there were two London and two Maidstone carriers, and another carrier whose journeys were unspecified. In 1823, waggons and vans passed through for London four times weekly, and there were vans and carts daily (except Sunday) for Maidstone. In 1836 William Jewhurst (a retired miller) said that 'I very often see the fish vans passing' from Hastings to London.

At the same date hops were sent to London in farmers' waggons and by carrier to get the best prices, because carriage by river, though at half the cost, was so much slower at two miles an hour. The

Introduction

An early nineteenth century engraving of the Town Hall and upper High Street, with the Rose and Crown on the right. The Hall was built by William Woodgate, the market owner and Lord of the Manor. Traders were sheltered by the Court Hall above. (Source: Tonbridge Historical Society)

growing town got more groceries and textiles from London and Maidstone, much being sent on to Tunbridge Wells and neighbouring rural parishes. From Tonbridge cattle market, one of the most important in Kent in the early nineteenth century, cattle and sheep were driven to London, though some sheep were sent by carcass to save loss of weight; London traders were 'induced to come into the country to buy' if supplies in the metropolis were short.

Coaches left the inns particularly for London, Hastings and the Wells, and also Brighton, Rye and Maidstone. The new seaside resorts and the expansion of the Wells increased passenger traffic dramatically. On 24 February 1824 the Maidstone Journal advertised a 'desirable residence' in Pembury near the Tonbridge-Hastings road 'where coaches pass six times daily'. In 1836 at least 20 coaches went through Tonbridge in both directions daily in summer.

One special factor was the coming of water transport to the town. In 1741 the Medway, previously navigable to Maidstone, was at last opened for trade to Tonbridge, which became the 'port' on the upper part of the river. A joint-stock company was formed by act of parliament which stressed the importance of the water carriage of

Wealden timber for naval dockyards such as Chatham. The share-holders were local property-owners and about £14,000 was spent clearing the river and building locks and wharves between Tonbridge and Maidstone. The Medway Navigation Company barges took timber, iron at first, hops and farm produce downstream from the town wharf and returned with coal (the most important good), imported softwoods for building, lime for farming and construction, stone and gravel; chalk was also carried and burnt at the Company kiln by the wharf. Dividends were paid almost continuously from 1749 and rose until the 1830s. When the Hon. John Byng stayed at the Rose and Crown Inn in 1788 they 'were ill at ease, it being filled by a company of all sorts belonging to the Medway navigation, who here held their annual dinner, and whom the ostler said were prieters [proprietors]'.

The prosperity that the commerce was bringing to the town soon attracted the attention of topographical writers. Hasted wrote in 1782 that 'as a result of the navigation the trade of the town has greatly increased'; this was accompanied by growth in the number and wealth of the inhabitants. Nearly every writer until the coming of the railways said the same. A H Neve wrote of the line of waggons laden with hops waiting in the High Street for the barge in the hop picking season in the 1830s, a visible symbol of the prosperity brought by river navigation. The Medway Company carried about 30,000 tons annually. It was the most important cause of the more rapid growth of Tonbridge than of other towns in south Kent, except the Wells. In 1664, the only date before 1841 when it is possible to compare urban populations approximately, Tonbridge was smaller than Westerham, Sevenoaks, Cranbrook and Ashford. In 1841 when exact calculations can be made from the manuscript census, Tonbridge (3,115) was three times the size of Westerham (1,191), twice that of Cranbrook (1,656), and larger than Sevenoaks (2,462) and even Ashford (3,082).

The society of the town is best considered about 1800, when evidence survives about both the more substantial inhabitants and the numerous paupers. In 1803 Finch's Directory of Kent lists 169 people,

Introduction

normally householders, of whom about 155 lived in the town and the rest in the vicinity. The townspeople were several gentry and the middle ranks of society, master craftsmen, tradesmen and professional men, comprising the most substantial one-third of the working people. The biggest group (55) were men engaged in light manufacturing; usually they employed apprentices and skilled or unskilled workmen who sold their goods or services.

Those involved in clothing included six tailors, but there were also three perukemakers (wigmakers), a milliner and a glover. Food preparation was done by two millers and five bakers. Two watchmakers practised their very skilled trade. There were nine building craftsmen (four carpenters), three working in leather and a tallow chandler. Seven men in woodwork included four turners, making the celebrated Tunbridge Ware. Furniture crafts included two cabinetmakers, a chairmaker and basketmaker. Four smiths and a farrier, a saddler, collarmaker and wheelwright were helping horse transport and farm work. Specialists in metal work and tools were a gunsmith, cutler and two braziers.

Trade was serviced by five carriers, a toll gatekeeper and a wharfinger. The shopkeeper group was large. There was a hatter and two linen-drapers. Food and drink comprised four butchers, four 'grocers etc', a wine merchant and seven victuallers (which included innkeepers). Two stationers and seven general shopkeepers represented the rest in this category. The bank had three partners, two landowners and a solicitor. Finally there were 25 men in the professions and public service. The law had a barrister and six attorneys, medicine a doctor, three surgeons and a druggist, and teaching two schoolmasters and a writing master. Religion was represented by three clergy (one dissenting), a parish clerk and sexton. A final miscellaneous group were the auctioneer, distributer of stamps and workhouse governor.

The town served the surrounding countryside in various ways. Some of the shopkeepers were wholesalers as well as retailers. When Thomas Beeching set up a large linen-draper's shop at the corner of Church Lane and the High Street in 1789 he began to advertise himself as 'salesman, linen-draper, mercer, hosier and hatter' with a rich variety of materials and clothing, 'country shops supplied and parishes served as usual', presumably to clothe paupers (Maidstone Journal, 24 May 1791). The villages had general shopkeepers, but farmers and gentlemen and their families were dependent on the town's more specialised tradesmen such as stationers and watchmakers. There was a skilled gunsmith. In 1778 (Kentish Gazette, 26-29 August) Samuel Ollive claimed to have 'invented a charger to deposit the gunpowder into the chamber of the barrel ... sold as low as Two Shillings each, with good allowance to those who sell again'. He was also a 'Clock and Watch Maker'. He was followed by Richard Fishenden who designed a butt for Sir Humphry Davy in 1813. The bank of Children, Woodgate and Scoones lasted from 1792 until its collapse in 1812. Another bank also fell, but Beeching ran a bank successfully from at least 1815.

The neighbourhood was particularly dependent on the profes-sional men. At the end of April 1778 a surgeon and man-midwife named Parsons who had trained in London advertised in the Kentish Gazette that he had opened a shop in Tonbridge High Street; to begin his trade he offered to 'deliver any poor woman gratis at, and within four miles of Tonbridge, during the space of three months'. The attorneys in particular served the surrounding countryside. A register of writs of covenant relating to conveyances (1779-1809) kept by the firm of Scoones, attorneys in East Lane, refers to property in various parishes mostly up to 10 or 15 miles away. Apart from conveying property, lawyers handled estates if the owner was unable to act himself, arranged loans and were clerks to turnpike trustees and stewards of local manors.

In addition to the shops and markets the leading inns drew people for business and entertainment such as meetings which probably on some occasions included petty sessions. Games with prizes, which probably included races (possibly sometimes in sacks or with wheel-barrows) and stool-ball for wage earners, and pigeon shooting matches for farmers and gentlemen were held in the town in the later eight-eenth century. On 5 October 1790 the Journal advertised a 'Shooting

Introduction

Match – The Annual Diversions at Tonbridge' to be held on Monday next 'for the convenience of farmers hiring servants', that is, the traditional hiring for a year of servants boarded with farmers; 'when many other articles, besides what is annually given, will be given gratis'; 'on the same day, a Shooting Match for a Silver Cup, and gentlemen competing are asked to meet at the Chequers at 9 a.m., to begin shooting precisely at 10 a.m.'. Plays were given by visiting actors in large inn rooms and other buildings. The attraction of the town for entertainment and company as well as business is shown by the residence of several gentry families, such as the Childrens at Ferox Hall, and women of independent means such as the three Woodgate sisters between 1790 and 1827 opposite the Chequers. As Margaret Stephens writes (page 163), other gentry lived within a mile of the town.

The middle orders owned the houses. The survey made in 1739 mentions 75 owners of about 180 dwellings. Only George Hooper had more than ten (19) and most owners held one, two or three tenements, often self-occupied. Small capitalists built and let cottages in the countryside. It is generally accepted that the English middle classes enjoyed improving living conditions in this period. For Tonbridge people in new or partly rebuilt houses bricks were fire-proof, durable and kept the heat in and cold out. Coal was available for heating. Shops and their goods were becoming more varied. More reading and knowledge of national events is shown by the presence of the Kentish Gazette in the town from 1769 and the Maidstone Journal after 1785. A Literary Institution was set up in 1836, with books and newspapers for subscribers. Their use was helped by better private schooling, discussed in detail by Dorothy Stammers (page 135) and Sally Hedley-Jones (page 147).

Increasing ownership of more expensive jewellery, clothing and other valuables is suggested by two attempts to form a night watch in 1812 and 1826, both years of severity for poorer people tempted to steal. On 11 February 1812 the Journal reported 'a general meeting of the inhabitants of Tonbridge Town, held at the Castle Inn' on 29 January, attended by nearly 150 people who formed themselves into 'an association and watch, for the purpose of protecting property from nightly depredations' with a committee of notables to organise a nightly watch. Entertainment, sport and visits to London and the seaside by the gentry in the later Georgian period are discussed by Peter Humphries (page 23).

Life improved less for the majority in England. The better paid artisans probably did best. Thus in Tonbridge parish three friendly societies with 100 members each existed in the 1810s. The delay in setting up a savings bank until 1845 in the town was no doubt the result of its relatively small size. The Town Wardens' records studied by Sydney Simmons (page 83) provide a local series of building wages. As elsewhere in the south wages rose sharply during the French Wars, and men joined the armed forces. Costs of food and building materials increased at least as much, bread prices catastrophically after bad harvests. Wage earners benefited only in the slump in prices from the mid-1810s (though unemployment grew) and from modestly rising real wages in the 1820s and 1830s. Local farm labourers in the 1820s were earning 8s or 10s weekly. In the early 1830s £30 was quoted as the annual average earning of a labourer; there was a little harvest and hop picking work for women and children, and older boys might add 2s or 3s a week to the family income. The wife had to be economical. At this time after rent, wood and flour there was a little money for potatoes, butter, tea, sugar, salt, pepper and weekly bacon. The rapidly expanding Wells needed more servants and other workers, but the resort could draw for labour on a large rural area in the Weald. In 1841 its well-to-do residents employed over 1,000 household servants, while Tonbridge town had 224.

Rising population from the 1750s in agricultural areas such as the Weald added to unemployment and underemployment. Poor rates jumped (Table 1.3). In the parish they were 14 times as much in 1834 as in 1750; yet the cost of living about doubled by 1814 and then fell and the population no more than quintupled between the mid-eighteenth century and 1834. In 1802-03, before allowing for probable double counting, 548 inhabitants (12 or 13 per cent of the total) were relieved either permanently or occasionally. The

Introduction

workhouse in Bank Street held 130 (the maximum) and the other
paupers had outdoor relief in the form of pensions, rent payments
etc. The parish was also holding 190 people from other parishes in
the large and old Peach Hall beyond the southernmost bridge and in
various cottages and alleys in the town. About 60 per cent of all the
paupers were under 15, and another 12 per cent were aged, sick or
disabled. Thus a little more than a quarter were able-bodied men
and women. They reveal in particular the inability of the farms to

Table 1.3: Poor Law expenditure in Tonbridge parish, 1750-1834

	£	s	d		£	s	d
1750	517	9	1	1803	2,831	12	4
1765	909	11	1	1813-15	5,153	0	0
1776	1,114	9	3	1823-25	4,551	1	0
1783-85	1,395	10	11	1833-35	7,079	0	0

use additional labour. The number of paupers varied as those needing occasional relief changed with the price of bread. After the bad
years of 1809-12 wheat prices fell in 1813, 1814, and 1815; in these
years ending at Easter occasional aid was given to 653, 478 and 196
respectively The parish charities and almshouses made a small contribution to relief. A little under £100 was available from charitable
bequests in the 1810s, and there were 10 almshouses. In times of
distress collections paid for gifts of meat, bread and fuel to poor
families.

In the 1830s the ancient parish ceased to be a community. Already
by 1750 the Wells was socially and economically independent of the
rest of the parish. By 1810 or 1820 its rapidly growing population
was becoming cut off from the rural influence natural in a centre of a
few hundred people. The ecclesiastical and administrative parish bonds
were broken between 1831 and 1844. Southborough became an
ecclesiastical parish in 1831, Holy Trinity, Tunbridge Wells in 1833
and Hildenborough in 1844. The Wells was given self-governing
powers in 1835. The strongest civil tie of the original parish was the
administration of the poor law, and the Poor Law Amendment Act

21

of 1834, which merged the parish with nine others for the purposes of relief, reduced its work enormously.

The writings of Beauchamp Wadmore, A H Neve, the Woodgate descendants, G P Hoole and other authors have contributed to the history of Georgian Tonbridge, and the following six essays with separate themes greatly augment our knowledge of the town and parish in the period.

Sources

Wadmore, B, *Some Details in the History of the Parish of Tonbridge* (1906)

Neve, A H, (1933, revised edition 1934)

Victoria History of the County of Kent III (1930)

Woodgate, G M G, *A History of the Woodgates of Stonewall Park and of Summerhill in Kent, and their Connections* (printed for private circulation, Wisbech, [1910])

Chalklin, C W, *A Kentish Wealden Parish (Tonbridge) 1550-1750,* (B.Litt. thesis, Oxford University, 1960)

Hoole, G P, *Sir Humphry Davy: Tonbridge Associations* (1978)

Hasted, E, *The History and Topographical Survey of Kent, Volume V,* (1798)

Finch, W, *Directory of Kent* (1803)

Kentish Gazette (1778)

Maidstone Journal (1785-1830: parts)

Parliamentary Papers 1803-04 XIII, 1818 XIX, 1822 V, 1825 IV, XIX, 1830-31 XI, 1834 XXX-XXXIII, 1836 XXIX

Centre for Kentish Studies: P371/8,12; U249 B1; U443 T8

House of Lords Record Office: South Eastern Railway Bill, minutes of evidence, 1836

Public Record Office: H.O. 107/462, 463, 471, 472, 485 (manuscript censuses, 1841)

The Landed and Propertied Classes of Georgian Tonbridge

Dr P L Humphries

In order to understand the workings of a community at any period of its history, it is essential to identify the driving dynamic and predominant ideas at the heart of economic, political, and social relations. Societies rarely stand still, though the pace of change may sometimes appear so languid as to be almost indiscernible. At other times, a century, a decade, or even a couple of years marks a decisive stride forward, admitting of no retreat, but impelling customs and cherished certainties into new and uncharted ways. Hence, in its earliest phase, the settlement at Tonbridge experienced a rapid growth, in W H Ireland's words, as 'suburbs belonging to the castle', where the populace 'partook of the vicissitudes of fortune of the castle and its lords'.[1] The household and garrison of the de Clare Earls of Gloucester provided employment for the inhabitants dwelling beneath the bailey walls, while the fortified motte acted as refuge in time of trouble.

A similar all-pervading surge took place during the nineteenth century, when Tonbridge found itself swept along upon the national tide of democratic, reforming, and utilitarian zeal, establishing numerous committees, boards, and finally a council, to regulate and superintend ever more aspects of communal life, and at every turn, confronting the radical, sometimes painful, challenges of 'Railway Mania', better public sanitation, and Free Trade. In the centuries between the collapse of feudal loyalties and the halcyon age of Victorian prosperity, the impetus for change pressed with less urgency, even if the Black Death, the Reformation, and the Civil Wars could scarcely fail to leave their indelible scars on inhabitants, buildings, and the landscape. During the eighteenth century, however, Tonbridge entered a vital phase of transition; a prelude, perhaps, to the greater

23

events after 1840, yet in its own right, no less dramatic or self-contained. On this occasion, the essential catalyst came not from some benign and powerful baron, but rather from the town's resident landed and propertied classes, whose influence, for more than a century, permeated every stratum of local affairs. The Tonbridge gentry – for as such will this essay choose loosely to define a broad but distinct group of inhabitants – represents, in its own right, a fascinating subject for study. It is necessary, in the first instance, to account for the appearance of this gentry on the Tonbridge stage; and, having done so, a range of primary and secondary source material may be quarried to support a detailed analysis of the gentry in terms of its composition and mechanics. More important still, for the historian of eighteenth-century Tonbridge, it is the interests and the activities, the strengths and weaknesses, the prejudices, aspirations, and philanthropy of this group, that serve to explain and illuminate the functioning and steady evolution of society. In administration and the law, in religion and private charity, in matters of rural and urban economy, in politics, and in the improving quality of life, the gentry families of Tonbridge continued, throughout the Georgian period, to play a crucial and decisive rôle, both in the van of progress and at the fulcrum of organisation and control.

The rise of the Tonbridge gentry

Professor G E Mingay begins a classic study in English social history with the assertion that: 'Landed property was the foundation of eighteenth-century society'; a thesis which he then substantiates with a wealth of evidence drawn from estate papers and other documentary evidence.[2] At the highest level of analysis, Mingay describes how great aristocratic families – Russell, Pelham, Cavendish, and their ilk – monopolise the offices and preferments of state, leaving the lesser nobility and gentry to exercise an almost uncontested influence across the shires, parishes, and hundreds, from Cornwall to Northumberland. In the county of Kent, the tradition of a proud and independent gentry was particularly strong and deeply rooted. There was, moreover, an absence of large aristocratic estates, and neither the Crown, the Church, nor government agencies owned sufficient property to wield more than a very localised predominance. Successive generations of Knatchbulls, Honywoods, Marshams, Twysdens, Filmers, Fanes, and Derings had voiced the county's opinions and contested its parliamentary representation since before the Civil Wars of the seventeenth century, and felt themselves the fortunate heirs of a people never subdued by the 'Norman yoke'. During the Georgian period, the strength and pervasive confidence of this landed interest was enhanced still further by the emergence of a class of lesser gentry, whose values and resources soon assumed a profound importance for the well-being of many rural and semi-urban Kentish communities.

The Tonbridge of the eighteenth century was such a community. As has been seen, the town's population grew steadily, especially from the 1750s, and there was a corresponding rise in the wealth and social status of many Tonbridge people. Whereas, in the seventeenth century, the vicar and his curate, the school master and usher, a lawyer, and several surgeons, alone represented a professional class, by the time that the historian and antiquary, Edward Hasted, published his *History and Topographical Survey of the County of Kent* towards the close of the next century, Tonbridge could boast a thriving indigenous gentry at the apex of its social pyramid.[3] Among a variety of reasons which might be advanced to account for this marked evolution in social composition, the extraordinary fluidity of the local land market, better communications, and the expansion of economic and leisure-time amenities, seem deserving of special attention, since it was their timely combination that in great measure explains why Tonbridge, rather than neighbouring Sevenoaks, made such rapid progress in the Georgian period.

During the first half of the seventeenth century, we find that about nine thousand acres in Tonbridge parish (about three fifths of the total) was in the control of four manorial demesnes. Then, quite dramatically, in the space of just half a century between the Restoration and the death of Queen Anne, the demise of the owning families brought all these estates under the hammer in quick succession.[4] The

manor of Tonbridge was partitioned in 1674 and 1676, when a
settlement was at last reached among the several heirs of the former
absentee proprietor, Sir Peter Vanlore. Parts of the Southborough
demesne were sold off after the death of Robert Smith in 1695,
while the Dachurst lands of the Skaffingtons began to come on to the
market after 1715. In South Frith, the cause of disintegration was
profligacy rather than lineal failure. The extravagant life-style of the
daughter and heiress of the Marquis of Clanricard finally left her son,
the Earl of Buckingham, no alternative but to mortgage and then
dispose of his five thousand acres during the years immediately
following 1700.

When it is recalled that South Frith alone accounted for a third of
the Tonbridge parish, it is not too wild an assertion to see in the
upheavals of the late seventeenth century, a repetition, albeit in
microcosm, of the social revolution which attended the dissolution
of monastic lands during the Reformation. Free at last to purchase
land, the farmers, freeholders, and yeomen of the area, together with
some prosperous metropolitan merchants, were able, over several
generations, to acquire significant properties, and in some notable
instances, soon aspired to genteel status. As early as 1677, a yeoman
named William Eldridge bought areas of the Postern recently released
from the demesne of Tonbridge, and fifty years later, in 1728, a
descendant consolidated the family patrimony by the addition of the
Postern Farm. The Wellers obtained numerous houses, farms, and
smaller parcels of land in the Postern, in Tunbridge Wells, and south
of the Medway, from both the manors of Tonbridge and South
Frith; while among others to benefit at this period may be included
the Walters, the Polhills of Otford, the Hoopers, and the Woodgates.

The social transformation proved irresistible, and continued
throughout the eighteenth century, even though the pace of land
sales inevitably slackened. Former tenants and copyholders soon ranked
as independent farmers; yeomen could expand small-holdings into
more viable agricultural units; and for the lesser gentry of neighbouring parishes, there was the opportunity to secure an interest in a town
whose economic prospects seemed set fair on a flood-tide of prosperity.

Equally important for the character of the Tonbridge gentry, the ownership of land did not turn full circle, as happened in some parts of the county, where the wealthiest family steadily bought out farmers and poorer squires to gain an overwhelming supremacy. Tonbridge never spawned a Sackville or a Cornwallis; but on the contrary, was to witness a fresh land dispersal when the extensive Children and Woodgate estates were sold off in the early nineteenth century.

More will be said about the growth of the Tonbridge economy in a later part of this study; it is instructive in the present context, however, to note that the opening up of the Medway in around 1740, to transport goods from the rural hinterland to Rochester, Chatham, and beyond, greatly accelerated the social trends of earlier decades. Timber was no longer the staple building material, since clay and lime for bricks, and even stone, could now be imported or manufactured locally at a fraction of previous expense and trouble. The full riches and variety of London shops and warehouses also became more accessible, to the great satisfaction of families of taste and fashionable inclination. Writing of Tonbridge in the latter half of the century, Hasted observes that: 'Since the river Medway has been made navigable up to it, the trade of it has been greatly increased, as well as the wealth and number of the inhabitants'. He notes the erection in recent times of 'many good houses', and remarks that 'several persons of genteel fortune' had been induced 'by so healthy and pleasant a situation' and 'a well supplied market' to take up permanent residence.[5]

The discovery, early in the seventeenth century, of restorative waters at a rural spot some miles to the south of Tonbridge, added a new dimension to the old town's desirability as a place of abode, especially as the Wells became more and more fashionable. During the early decades of the spa, it was usual for visitors to lodge in the houses of the locals, and only around 1700 did purpose-built accommodation become readily available. When Celia Fiennes stayed at Tunbridge Wells in 1694, she found the resort still reasonably cheap and unsophisticated; there were coffee houses, exercise walks, and a market, with water being drawn from the natural spring.[6] Daniel

Defoe encountered 'the nobility and gentry of the country' in abundance, during his tour in about 1720, although, having noted the profusion of facilities on offer, he felt compelled to remark that 'without money a man is a no-body at Tunbridge'.[7] Writing about fifty years later – by which time the spa had matured still further as a centre of cultivation and pleasure – Charles Seymour pens a most attractive portrait of the place, describing the waters as 'of great efficacy in colds, chronical distempers, weak nerves and bad digestion'.[8]

Coaches regularly traversed the newly-turnpiked routes from London to the Wells, carrying passengers, mail, and provisions of all kinds. Finch's *Directory of Kent*, published in 1803, reflects the emergence of this basic infrastructure, including among its entries for Tonbridge, a gate-keeper, five carriers (two on the London road and one on the Maidstone road), and W Steer, the deputy postmaster. Inns like the Angel, the Rose and Crown, and the Bull, could furnish horses and chaises, as well as dinners and beds for touring parties. An influx of well-to-do residents was the natural consequence for Tonbridge, giving an air of affluence to the descriptions of contemporary authors such as Charles Seymour, who writes of 'one broad street, adorned by some very good modern houses' in the 1770s.[9]

During the eighteenth century, therefore, a landed and propertied class had arrived in Tonbridge and coalesced quickly into a sizeable, articulate, and fairly homogeneous social grouping, with a distinctive and visible presence in the town. Land was generally the prime inducement, although other factors, both economic and recreational, doubtless acted as additional recommendations. This new Georgian gentry could trace its ancestry to perhaps three or four principal sources: to established county families, usually via younger sons or cadet branches, to metropolitan merchants, to prosperous local yeomen farmers, and often to successful professionals. The Woodgates, the Hookers, the Childrens, and the Austens correspond respectively to these broad categories, and it is to them and their ilk, to their ideals, and to their web of social relationships, that attention must now shift, if we are to understand how and why the gentry shaped the course and character of Tonbridge affairs for more than a century.

The composition of the Tonbridge gentry

No source for a definition of the Georgian gentry, and the social environment in which it flourished, could be more contemporary or more authentic than Jane Austen; and especially so in the present context, since throughout her life, she enjoyed close family ties with Tonbridge. In *Persuasion*, a novel where the recurring theme of rank and social inter-relations is exemplified in the opening chapter, we find the fairly representative opinion that the true gentry was composed of those not obliged to follow any profession, but who could live 'in a regular way, in the country, choosing their own hours, following their own pursuits, and living on their own property, without the torment of trying for more'. The Musgroves and the financially-embarrassed Elliots fall squarely into this category, as do the families of Bennet, Woodhouse, Bertram, and Knightley, to mention just a handful of well-loved names from elsewhere in the canon. As to the personal characteristics of the gentleman, the qualities mistakenly ascribed to William Walter Elliot are evidently those most prized in Jane Austen's day. He is spoken of as possessing a 'good understanding', 'correct opinions', and 'strong feelings of family attachment and family honour'; and, in addition to liberality, judgement, and unselfishness, is warmly applauded for retaining a 'value for all the felicities of domestic life'.

Like Sir Walter Elliot, the gentry as a class knew and valued its history and established place in English society. The titled aristocracy topped the social pyramid, distinguished by coronet from baron up to royal duke. Next, the baronets, in order of creation precedence, and then the knights, upon whom honours were conferred for a single life. Among the mass of the squirearchy, no less than among its social superiors, an awareness of birth and position rated as highly as any entry in the peerage or baronetage. Hence, the Elliots, Musgroves, and Hayters of Kellynch and Uppercross give and receive the distinctions due to their respective houses; living, marrying, and walking into dinner in solemn accordance with family status.

Ever conscious of its own identity, the Georgian gentry retained equally definite opinions about the status and civilities due to the other ranks within society. Members of the clerical, legal, military, and medical professions, however wealthy, sacrificed full gentility on the altar of daily toil; while for those like Mrs Elton and the Coles in *Emma*, whose fortune originated in trade, acceptance and equality within the gentry might take a generation or more to accomplish. As to the 'profit and loss' farmers, it is deemed to be quite impossible and inappropriate for a Miss Woodhouse of Heartfield to remain the friend and confidant of a Mrs Robert Martin, no matter how diligent and worthy might be the tenant of Abbey-mill farm.

But, if on first acquaintance the Georgian gentry appears innately conservative and strictly regimented, a glance at the community and *dramatis personae* of *Emma* quickly serves to emphasise its flexibility and tolerance at a provincial level. The Knightleys of Donwell Abbey and the Woodhouses of Heartfield are the acknowledged superiors of Highbury, owning land and good houses, and linked by marriage and mutual interests. Mr Woodhouse represents the junior branch of an ancient family, with sufficient wealth to give his daughters dowries of £30,000. The Westons of Randalls come next in the hierarchy, followed by several other families still labouring to convert mercantile coin into pure, unsullied, genteel gold. The resident vicar, Mr Elton, is a welcome visitor to every drawing-room, and the better professional families regularly gain admittance to balls and other communal entertainments. The proprietress of the local girls' school is within the Heartfield circle, and even the relative poverty of Mrs Bates and her talkative daughter cannot place these dependants of a former vicar beyond the pale of polite society. For the younger son of Donwell, there is a legal career in London, while for Emma's governess to become mistress of Randalls seems a quite proper elevation for a woman of good sense and agreeable manners. Clearly, the eighteenth-century gentry was a complex organism, not easy to define or circumscribe, yet possessed of great and distinctive influence, which the historian disregards at his peril.

Who, then, were the men and women of Georgian Tonbridge's landed and propertied gentry, the equivalents in real life of Jane

Austen's fictional parade? In answering this question, an invaluable documentary source is available in the form of the town's land tax assessments for the period 1780 to 1832. The land tax was levied upon the rentable value of all kinds of property, ranging from simple dwelling houses, gardens, yards, and meadows, to farms, business premises, warehouses, wharves, and even tithes. The extant lists in the Centre for Kentish Studies display proprietor, occupier, and amount of assessment; and, when supplemented by information from directories, maps, and other surviving material, give a good idea of who constituted the property owners in the immediate vicinity of the town centre.

The 1780 assessment records taxable property in the possession of 44 persons, while the 1800 list details 86 proprietors. As might be expected, a considerable number of properties were in the hands of a small group of individuals. In 1780, some 50 per cent of the proprietors had more than one property, a percentage which is repeated in the 1800 assessment. The ownership of property also tended to be confined to local families. Fourteen of the 1780 proprietors, and 34 of the 1800 proprietors, resided in their own houses, and a sizeable proportion of the remainder may be identified as dwelling either in the town or its near environs.

The precise social status of these property owning classes, and the likely levels of their incomes, is not easy to determine. The valuations from which land tax assessments derived, were only revised on a periodic basis, while in the semi-urban context of Georgian Tonbridge, we are dealing with a varied class of proprietors, whose earnings might well stem from a mixture of land and house rents, professional fees, and a host of commercial enterprises. At the top end of the social spectrum, Professor Mingay estimates that towards the end of the eighteenth century, the greater gentry families of knights and baronets enjoyed revenues of £3,000 to £4,000 per annum, the middle ranks of esquires from £1,000 to £3,000, while incomes of the lesser gentry might range from £300 to £1,000.[10] Unlike its near neighbour, Tonbridge was scarcely large enough or sufficiently fashionable to attract members of the titled gentry within its borders; however, both of the land tax assessments do distinguish several names with the courtesy of 'Esq'. In the 1780 list, Thomas Hooker and William Woodgate appear in this category, alongside the well-known Kentish names of Honywood and Polhill. The tithe-owning Honywoods are again among the esquires in the 1800 assessment, and William Woodgate is joined by William Francis Woodgate, John Woodgate, and George Children. Finch's 1803 directory lists nine esquires among its entries for Tonbridge: W F and F Woodgate, George and J G Children, J H West, W Simmons, Mr Selater, and W S and W T Harvey.

As leading inhabitants of Tonbridge over several generations, the Hookers, Woodgates, and Childrens seem to merit some further words of introduction. The Hookers, for instance, were the descendants of Sir William Hooker, who became Lord Mayor of London in 1675, and of his son, John Hooker of West Peckham, the High Sheriff of Kent in 1712. The two sons of this latter – Thomas and John – settled in Tonbridge and Brenchley respectively; and a grandson, the celebrated John Hooker, consolidated the fortunes of the Tonbridge branch when he married Elizabeth, heiress of John Wood, and granddaughter of John Petley. Having obtained much property in the Slade area through his wife, John Hooker bought the castle, manor, and demesne of Tonbridge from Henry Zinzan in 1739. As proprietor of the Medway Navigation Company, Hooker again enhanced his status in the town, and could afford to build Fosse Bank House as his principal residence. Thomas Hooker succeeded to his father's titles and estates in 1779, and in 1793 he initiated the construction of a 'handsome stone mansion' next to the castle ruin. Though Hooker left Tonbridge soon after this date, his Brenchley cousins maintained a footing in local affairs, and frequently appear as friends and correspondents of the Woodgates. By the eighteenth century, the transformation of the Children family from substantial yeomen to professional and propertied gentry was complete. Owning properties in Bordyke and the Hadlow Road area, as well as rural holdings in Leigh and elsewhere, John Children consummated his relations with Tonbridge by the purchase of Ferox Hall in 1750. His family already had ties of marriage with the Woodgates, and he himself took Jane Weller as his bride. George Children built upon the foundations laid by his father; he greatly extended his social and professional connection among the Tonbridge gentry, and by further purchases in Hildenborough, Leigh, and other adjoining parishes, expanded his estate to between 2,000 and 3,000 acres. After 1800, Ferox Hall became the scene of pioneering chemical experimentation, inspired by young John George Children, who later travelled widely and achieved high renown as a man of science.

The story of the Woodgates in the early eighteenth century bears many similarities to that of the Hookers. Elected as High Sheriff of Kent in 1700, William Woodgate hailed from a well-established gentry family, with roots deep in the wooded acres around Penshurst. His son, John Woodgate, came to Tonbridge in 1712, where, with the rich and beautiful Rose Birsty as his bride, he added Somerhill and its lands to those of his patrimony. Henry Woodgate inherited both Somerhill and Stonewall Park in 1728; but in 1769, he allowed the management of all his properties to pass to his nephew, William Woodgate, whose father, the Revd Francis Woodgate, was a younger son of John and Rose Woodgate, and had for many years enjoyed the living of Mountfield. William Woodgate was a shrewd man; a man whose energy and acumen brought wealth to a hitherto somewhat neglected estate, ensured generous provision for a large family, and secured for the master of Somerhill, a wide-ranging influence over the life and opinions of his adopted town. When he died in 1809, Woodgate had amassed a fortune worth £300,000, and could bequeath sums of between £30,000 and £50,000 to his four sons, and portions of £10,000 to each of his daughters.[11] As the century proceeded, the Woodgate presence in Tonbridge town grew markedly. Old Henry Woodgate occupied a house on the main street until his death in 1787, while in 1790, William Woodgate's three sisters – Miss Ann, Miss Sarah, and Miss Rose – settled in the town after the death of their father. In 1793, William Woodgate purchased Thomas Hooker's new house beside the castle, where, in the next year, he installed his eldest son, William Francis, known locally as the

William Francis Woodgate, 1770–1828; he succeeded to the Castle and Somerhill in 1809, but was forced to sell his Kent estates after the collapse of the Tonbridge Bank in 1812–16. (Source: Tonbridge Historical Society)

Major. Sadly for the long-term survival of the family, the sons of Somerhill, in particular its heir and his brother Henry, lacked the discernment of their father, being more disposed to play the fine gentlemen and to cut a dash among their neighbours. As will be seen, these failings ultimately led Major Woodgate to total ruin in 1816, and Henry was probably only preserved from a similar fate, firstly by two wealthy marriages, and then by his own premature death in 1818 following a riding accident. Despite these personal disasters, however, the century-long association between Tonbridge and the Woodgate clan was prolonged for a further generation, when, in 1820, Francis Woodgate, the son of Henry Woodgate of Riverhill and grandson of Francis Woodgate of Mountfield, purchased Ferox Hall, where he lived as an independent gentleman until his death in 1843.

The Woodgates are a prime example of an established Kentish family attracted into Tonbridge at the height of the land boom, while in the success of the Childrens and Hookers, we should see the parallel emergence of powerful gentry interests from yeoman and mercantile backgrounds. Thomas Hooker was the owner of two properties on the 1780 land tax return, and Henry, William, and Ann Woodgate possessed a total of seven taxable units, including the clapper meads and the priory meads. By the time the 1800 assessment was prepared, Thomas Hooker had moved into Hampshire, leaving much of his interest in the hands of the Woodgates. William Woodgate's name appears against 12 house or meadow properties, and that of his eldest son beside a further three. The castle house cost Major Woodgate £9 5s, and his town lands were assessed at some 30 shillings. In the 1800 list, George Children is recorded as the owner of eight properties, among which he paid £9 10s for Ferox Hall.

Having thus dealt with the more illustrious of the Tonbridge property-owning gentry, it is also necessary to make some mention of the diverse and important group of essentially urban-based proprietors enumerated on the land tax assessments. Mrs Weller Pooley, for instance, is described as the owner of six properties in 1780, and of eight in 1800. David and Thomas Shirlock appear against a combined tally of nine units in 1780, and of eleven in the record taken twenty years later. Other persons of substance in the 1780 list include Thomas Twort, William and Thomas Scoones of Swan Lane, Mrs Oliver, Samuel Peckham, Jacob Mercer, and Henry Sidney. By 1800, the Wise, Chalklin, and Eldridge families had also acquired multiple property holdings, and it is clear that men such as Samuel Mills and his son, Mr Muggridge, Mr Simmonds, and Mr Creasy were figures of consequence among their neighbours and tenants (and three of them reappear in the essay on p. 163). Many of the surnames mentioned in this paragraph appear in Finch's directory, among the 14 men designated as 'gentleman', alongside the additional names of Headland, Kipping, London, Wells, and West. The same source also identifies nine 'independent ladies'; some, like Mrs Eldridge and Mrs Harvey, the widows of local gentlemen, and others – Mrs Brampton, Mrs Cheeseman, Mrs Jeffery, and Mrs Punn – perhaps the relics of prosperous tradesmen or professional practitioners.

No survey of the provincial gentry would be complete without some reference to the resident lawyers, doctors, and clergymen, all of whom occupied important niches in the structure of Georgian society. Often related by birth or marriage to the gentry, their professional duties uniquely bridged the divide between property owners and the other social orders. Many Woodgate younger sons pursued careers in the Law and the Church, and John Children's daughter Ann married a London surgeon named Richard Davenport. On another level, the urban professions acted as a channel through which ambitious and enterprising individuals might achieve the wealth and contacts necessary for anyone who aspired to social mobility and gentility.

The Hooper family were lawyers in Tonbridge from the sixteenth century, occupying for many years 'Powells' in Swan Lane, and latterly possessing landed property in the Cage area (See p. 172). The attorney Thomas Swayne was the owner of the Manor House in Dry Hill during the latter part of the eighteenth century, and George Children himself pursued a career as a barrister before inheriting Ferox Hall in 1771. The Wellers, too, had risen by way of the legal profession, so much so that Robert Weller could aspire to the office of High Sheriff of Kent in 1728. Stephen Alchin, another lawyer and heir to the Hooper possessions, is recorded as the owner of six properties in both the land tax assessments of 1780 and 1800, and William Scoones, lawyer of Swan Lane, has no fewer than eleven properties against his name in the later survey. Finch's *Directory of Kent* lists six Tonbridge attorneys, and it is particularly instructive that men such as Fuzzard and Lutterell should have been accorded the distinction of gentleman.

Thomas Hankins, like his father, was a surgeon of Sevenoaks and Tonbridge, and before his death in 1807, had taken up residence at Dry Hill House. Other physicians were to rise as high, or indeed higher, in an age that saw the son of the King's doctor made successively Speaker and Prime Minister in Downing Street. Lutterell and Slatter appear as surgeons in 1803; Dr Brown and Dr West were practising in about 1830; while the name and reputation of Dr Gorham lived long in the affections of his patients and neighbours.

The Anglican Church filled a central place in the corporate life of Georgian towns, even though its theology and devotions had widely stagnated, and in spite of the popular appeal of John Wesley. The parish pulpit continued as a primary source for the dissemination of news and opinions, while throughout this period, the clergy was closely linked with all manifestations of education and charity. For much of the eighteenth century, the advowson of Tonbridge (the right to present a clergyman to the living) was in the possession of the Fane family of Hadlow Place, and then, after the death of Viscount Fane in 1789, passed to David Papillon of Acrise near Dover. Preferment to the living of Tonbridge afforded yet one more opportunity for a leading local family to influence the temper, conduct, and ideas of the whole community, and at the same time to secure the livelihood and social standing of a younger son, needy kinsman, or talented protégé. We should not, therefore, be surprised to find a Revd Mr Papillon ensconced at the Tonbridge vicarage by the end of the eighteenth century, just as, at about the same time, William Woodgate presented his son Stephen to the living of Pembury, having previously purchased the advowson for this very purpose in 1788.

Further bonds between the clergy and the provincial gentry might be forged through marriage. Susanna Jordan, daughter of the rector of Barming, became the wife of George Children. Thomas Mercer of the 180-acre Green Trees estate married the daughter of the Revd Henry Harpur, as, earlier in the century, Thomas Harvey of Hilden had allied himself to a daughter of the Revd William Davis. Valued alike in polite drawing-room and humble cottage, the clergyman, like the lawyer and the doctor, stood astride the social divide, widening the perspective of the gentry and fashioning the conduct of his whole flock.

The story of the Austens may serve to underline the crucial rôle fulfilled by the professions in the development of the gentry. Several branches of the family had evolved by the Georgian period, following the acquisition of considerable wealth in the cloth trade. When, however, the spendthrift John Austen of Horsmonden died prematurely in 1704, his wife, the former Elizabeth Weller, found herself in straitened circumstances. The three sons of this union took up careers in Tonbridge or Sevenoaks: William as a surgeon, Thomas as an apothecary, and Francis as a lawyer. Francis Austen was a typical eighteenth-century man of business, who built up a lucrative legal practice, and frequently acted on behalf of the Duke of Dorset. Two marriages brought Austen substantial property holdings, and to these he added lands in Dartford, Sevenoaks, Goudhurst, and West Wickham, giving him a reputed income of £6,000 by his death in 1791. Of the next generation, George Austen – son of William and father of the novelist, Jane Austen – enjoyed the patronage of his lawyer uncle and attended Tonbridge School, where he returned for a spell as second master in 1759, after taking Holy Orders and studying at St John's College, Oxford. Henry Austen, son of Thomas, was also educated at Tonbridge School and then at Cambridge, before being ordained as an Anglican clergyman. His marriage, as will be seen, linked Henry with many of the established gentry families of Tonbridge, and, after his adoption of Socinian views, he chose to seek retirement in a house just north of the Great Bridge. Within the span of a hundred years, the Austens had acquired a secure place in the Tonbridge gentry. Patiently and painstakingly, as medicine or the law or the cloth brought growing prosperity, a new generation built upon the successes of its fathers, marrying better, buying land, and becoming at length woven into the very fabric of local life. Established in his mansions at Kippington and Lamberhurst, Francis Motley Austen quickly shuffled off the professional drudgery that had engrossed his father's days, leaving his clerks and deputies to dance attendance at innumerable trusts and committees – the son of the Sevenoaks attorney had scaled the greasy pole, to achieve the ease of a country squire.

The gentry connection

Clearly the Tonbridge gentry, in all its kaleidoscopic complexity, belonged to that quintessentially Georgian amalgam so memorably depicted by Jane Austen. Her characters, like the scattered and varied cousinhood of Annes and Williams, Henrys, Johns, and Roses who animate the papers of the Woodgate clan, illustrate all the qualities and dispositions that made the gentry so pervasive an influence in its eighteenth-century heyday. It constituted a distinct stratum of English life, small enough to recognize and cherish its own pedigree and traditions, and yet possessed of a flexibility which tolerated the gradual augmentation of its ranks with men of talent and new wealth. The gentry was united by education, by a common inheritance, and by a tacit understanding of acceptable ethics and required social behaviour and responsibility. Hence, when we seek, in the remainder of this study, to document the rôle of the propertied classes in Georgian Tonbridge, we must begin our search for an explanation of its strength and all-embracing vitality, not in external ideology or artificial party structures, but rather in the minute interplay of personal and family relations, in the confused and confusing web of obligation and interest surrounding the ownership of property, and in the maintenance and exercise of influence in the economy, and through all available instruments of administration. Eighteenth-century commentators understood this phenomenon in terms of the creation and wide-ranging operation of 'connections'. The word and the ideas it embodies spring constantly from the pages of *Persuasion* and *Emma*; and, on a far grander scale, as Sir Lewis Namier has painstakingly demonstrated, it was upon the manipulation of a bewildering interplay of aristocratic connections, that Walpole and the Duke of Newcastle secured the Whig supremacy of George II's reign.[12] The essential strength and cohesion of the classic Whig connection emanated from an almost preternatural loyalty among kith and kin, made stronger still through the sinews and muscles of patronage and obligation, which stretched out to embrace many individuals, families, and interests within the wider body politic, sustaining, thereby, an entity with the will and the capacity to guarantee parliamentary majorities, to bargain with ministers, and even to shake the throne itself. The pattern and the practice remain constant when we focus on even the smallest provincial communities; and it may therefore be helpful to illustrate briefly the various levels at which a gentry-based connection might manifest itself in and about a town such as Tonbridge.

In the first instance, a connection founded on kinship frequently linked gentry families in a host of districts and urban centres. William Woodgate, for example, had connections with the Childrens and the Swaynes through the marriages of his two aunts, had strong ties with the Ashburnhams of Broomham in Sussex and the Humphrys of Seal, and was himself the son-in-law of John Hooker. His eldest son married Anna Allnutt, and his eldest daughter, Frances, married Richard Allnutt of South Park, Penshurst. A second daughter, Anne, married Peter Nouaille of Great Ness, Sevenoaks, while Maria allied herself to John Hartrup West of Postern Park. Of his younger sons, John remained a bachelor at Stonewall Park, whereas Stephen married Frances Hardinge – whose two brothers were, respectively, a vicar of Tonbridge, and Sir Charles Hardinge, the eminent diplomat – and Henry became successively the son-in-law of Lord Boyne of Tunbridge Wells and the Revd Thomas Harvey of Redleafe, Penshurst. Cousins from all these houses held posts in the law, the army, the church, and as merchants and men of letters, living in London and at the Universities. The network of interests so constructed proved invaluable in every aspect of public and private life, but became particularly visible at election times and during periods of war or social distress, when it was possible to mobilise opinion or relief, far beyond the scope of government or established institutions.

Connections based upon close family bonds and a commonality of economic preoccupations were also of vital importance among the property owners of towns like Tonbridge, where an oligarchy of leading families regularly renewed its ties at the parish altar. Nowhere is this better exemplified than in the marriage alliances forged by the three daughters of John Hooker. One of the sisters, Frances, married William Woodgate in 1769; another, Mary, united herself with Henry Austen; and a third, Elizabeth, first became the wife of Richard Children (brother of John Children and uncle of George) and later married Joseph Selater, the London lawyer. Viewed against such a back-cloth, William Woodgate's acquisition of the manor of

Tonbridge in 1793, and the permanent removal of Thomas Hooker, was less a disruptive sale, than a transfer of property and interest between brothers, which effectively preserved social continuity. Likewise, when business opportunities arose, or the town had to be roused to the threat of French invasion, it was natural for the Somerhill and Ferox Hall families to unite in a common purpose, made stronger and more enduring by kinship and fraternal solidarity. Finally, the connection may be viewed as a positive factor in binding together all sorts and degrees of people across Georgian society, from the aristocrat or the squire at the 'big house', down to his humblest tenant. Such relationships are less easy to document, being derived from an infinite variety of ties, including kinship, employment, preferment to office, and business interests, not forgetting simple gratitude and genuine respect. Consider, for just a moment, the potential scope of that extended connection preserved by the Sackvilles of Knole, and in particular, by the Duke of Dorset. His Grace was connected by birth and by marriage to many of his fellow Whig grandees, received political office at the hands of Walpole and the Pelhams, enjoyed considerable influence at Court and in Ireland, and served for many years as Lord Lieutenant of Kent. Yet, if the Sackvilles flourished like roses about the citadel of state, they were but the most visible adornments upon an organism whose tightly interwoven branches rambled and twisted sideways and downwards through so many fine gradations into the rich clays of the Weald.

The Sackvilles employed a trusted steward to oversee the ducal estates, retained the legal and administrative services of men like Francis and Francis Motley Austen, and could rely on the support of clergymen such as Dr Thomas Curteis, the rector of Sevenoaks and Wrotham. These professional men proved just as adept at connection-building as their social superiors, and perhaps for this reason, if for no other, penetrated the ranks of the gentry with some regularity. The doctor might count upon his interest among the druggists and apothecaries, as well as among his patients and fellow physicians; while for the clergyman to cultivate a persuasive influence over the sexton, the parish clerk, and the poorhouse keeper, appeared as a natural extension of his temporal ministry. Francis Austen, though he pursued his legal vocation until his death in 1791, was a rich man in his own right, with a personal connection to orchestrate on the Duke's behalf. He had links with David Papillon, the Farnabys, and the Leonards among the Kentish gentry, with Viscount and Viscountess Falkland, and with cousins like Sir Robert Austen and those in Tonbridge and Steventon. Austen had the livings of Chevening and West Wickham in his gift; he might also draw upon and reward the loyalty of his junior partners, his clerks, and his tenants, who, by virtue of their known associations with the client of a 'Great Man', might in their turn have a word to say, or an extra sixpence to spend, among their tradesmen and neighbours. Thus, in a myriad ways, did the eighteenth-century connection contrive to equate the interests of the lowest with the cause of the great and powerful.

The idea of the connection was the rock on which the entire eighteenth-century edifice rested, and as such, represents the unique element in a full understanding of Georgian Tonbridge. As will be made clear hereafter, the gentry of Tonbridge found itself called upon to participate in many spheres of local life; it was therefore constantly able to widen and utilise its connections in areas which bolstered its own status, and, at the same time, enabled the town to capitalise upon the opportunities of an age of unusual flux and diversity.

The gentry and the local economy

In the pre-industrial economy of Georgian Tonbridge, the rôle of the propertied classes was paramount. As owners of substantial domestic establishments within the town and upon its fringes, the local gentry filled an important position as consumers of goods and services, and as employers of a variety of labour. As landowners and landlords, the gentry provided leadership for the agricultural interest, and exercised a profound influence over the lives of urban and rural tenants alike. And, as owners of raw materials and capital, the gentry proved, as the eighteenth century matured, increasingly keen and able to fund and support new commercial enterprises. Hence, while the present study eschews any attempt to survey the pattern of estate and farm ownership, it does seek to illustrate some of the many ways in which the presence and activities of a propertied class helped to sustain and develop the economic life of Tonbridge. In so doing, it quickly becomes clear that the potency of family connections directly reflected the prevailing financial and proprietorial predominance of the gentry. So long as this correlation could be preserved intact, then, in Professor Mingay's words, the 'owners of the soil derived from its consequence and wealth the right to govern'.[13] Only later did the mirror crack, leaving on its shattered surface just the partial images of a way of life out-stripped by the sheer speed and ruthlessness of headlong progress.

The gentry houses of Georgian Tonbridge ranged in size and splendour from the 'large and venerable mansion' of Somerhill, to the more modest urban dwellings clustered along Bordyke, Swan Lane, and on Dry Hill.[14] Some might date their origins to the Tudor and Jacobean centuries, or even earlier, whereas others bore testimony to recent wealth in an era of more and cheaper building materials. Throughout the eighteenth century, the desire to build and decorate its properties in accordance with the latest fashion amounted almost to a mania among the English gentry. John Hooker was at work upon his first brick house in the 1730s, while at the turn of the century, James Burton began the construction of Mabledon to the south of the town, and George Children built The Mount in Hildenborough. Ferox Hall was one of many houses to experience major re-design during the period, receiving a new facade soon after its purchase by John Children. William Woodgate found himself obliged to undertake substantial repairs and improvements at Somerhill, and in later life incurred much expense in renovating Spring Grove and the vicarage in Pembury for his sons Henry and Stephen.[15]

House building and improvements usually went hand in hand with the laying out of parks and formal gardens, often with the addition of a strip of water or a ruined temple on some distant eminence. This was, after all, the age of Capability Brown and

Humphrey Repton, whose expertise, if it could not be afforded in person, might at least be imitated. Local builders, brick-layers, and masons, like those in the Mercer family of Tonbridge, all benefited from this abiding passion, as did the carpenters, cabinet-makers, and others engaged in the supply and fitting of interior decorations. Where London led, the provinces strove to follow; and if the squire or his lady espoused smart fashions, then so too did the doctor, the lawyer, and even the well-to-do farmer.

As the Tonbridge gentry built and enlarged its houses and gardens, there was a corresponding increase in the demand for domestic labour, with household and outdoor posts supplying employment for a considerable proportion of the local population. Butlers and footmen, housekeepers, cooks, and maids of all degrees, staffed the kitchens, served at table, and spent long hours cleaning and polishing those endless yards of passageways and staircases, carrying water and coals, and fulfilling the numberless functions of scullery, parlour, and dressing-room. Outside, a garden might resemble a veritable ant's nest of bustle, while the coachmen and grooms danced constant attendance in stable and harness-room. A cook with eight years experience might command four guineas a year, a housekeeper about £10, and a steward from £25 to £40, while for the orphan daughter of Henry Woodgate of Spring Grove, the Wests engaged a governess at £100 a year to teach French, Italian, music, dancing, and drawing.[16] In addition to the costs of household servants, the typical gentry family spent a sizeable portion of its income on the consumption of a large volume of locally-produced food and drink, hardware, clothing, and sundry personal and leisure-time accessories. Only the wealthiest landowners could retain a home farm to supply the kitchen and the larder, so that from the majority, shopkeepers such as the Jefferys, the Lucks, the Boxs, and the Featherstones, Barton the butcher, the bakers, the fishmonger, the fruiterer, and Bouvier the wine merchant, could rely on a regular demand for their produce. Likewise, the blacksmith and the wheelwright, cooper and gunsmith, makers of collars and harnesses, drapers, hatters, shoe-makers, tailors, and the peruke-maker were among a host of craftsmen who relied on the patronage of their gentry neighbours as a vital source of income and prosperity. Agriculture naturally formed the principal activity for the local population, since, either as farmers, foresters, or labourers, or indirectly through one of the numerous supporting crafts and processing trades, the great majority shared an interest in the well-being of the land. As described earlier, Tonbridge formed the focus of a large agricultural hinterland. Hasted writes of 'very fertile and good fatting land', especially in the lush water meadows of the Medway flood-plain; and goes on to remark that 'much of it is productive of good crops of corn and hops, of which there are several plantations'.[17] Markets were held weekly and monthly for the sale of poultry and cattle, while, even before the improvements of the eighteenth century, Tonbridge was the natural point from which to begin the transportation of produce by road or river. In addition, the area contained the remnants of the ancient forests of North Frith and South Frith, with sizeable acreages of oak extending to Southborough and Hildenborough.

The gentry owed its position and influence in this type of agrarian society, firstly to its own possession of land, and then to its ability to retain the leadership and confidence of the wider landed interest. Finch's *Directory of Kent* lists eight Tonbridge farmers in 1803, among them the names of Larkins, Duggen, Wright, Mills, and Gower. These were influential men in their own right; employers of labour, often with brothers and cousins engaged as cordwainers, tanners, or sawyers, and in their own rural sphere, as important to the gentry connection as the doctor or the lawyer in the town. For much of the eighteenth century, the claims and aspirations of the gentry, the independent yeomen freeholders, and the tenant farmers were preserved in a general state of equilibrium. Each group knew its own obligations and responsibilities, and it was only in periods of extreme agrarian distress, such as the late 1770s and again after 1800, that opinions began to diverge.

For the more substantial gentry, the principal source of income flowed normally from properties like Tile House Farm, Peach Farm, and Priory Farm, all of which belonged to the Somerhill estate south of the Medway. Among less well-to-do families, however, it was not uncommon for a master to work his own land, using horses between the shafts of plough and carriage according to the dictates of pleasure, business, or the seasons. Revenue might also be derived from tithes, although this was necessarily restricted to a few fortunate lay proprietors. John Hooker, for example, enjoyed the fruits of Hayesden and Little Barden, Matthew Smith those of Hilden, and James Eldridge those of the Postern. Sir John Honywood collected his dues from Tonbridge town, while the wards of Bourn Mill and Southborough accrued to Henry Goodwin and John Broadhurst respectively. In 1800, William Woodgate spent £1,782 on tithe rights in Southborough, South Frith, and elsewhere, with every expectation of obtaining, not only profits, but considerable influence over the farmers who tilled the soil.[18]

To achieve the successful management of an estate, the gentry landlord depended on a shrewd head for business and the ability to sustain a working relationship with his tenants. In prosperous times, the tenant would be expected to provide the capital to stock his farm, and to pay the land tax and the poor-rates. When crops failed or prices fell, however, it was often necessary for the gentry to shoulder some of these burdens, and to adopt a restrained attitude to the prompt payment of rents. William Woodgate estimated that 'the very necessary Qualifications for a desirable Tenant' were possessed by one who would 'use the Land well, & pay his Rent in due time'; and in a number of surviving letters, is revealed in the midst of spirited negotiations over timber and lease transactions.[19]

The gentry also assumed the responsibility for the spread of new ideas, and took the lead when the agricultural interest came under threat from outside. Only a Townshend or a Coke could really afford to pioneer the boldest innovations; but it regularly fell to the lesser squires to propagate the gospel of improvement. Arthur Young wrote articles and pamphlets with these very men in view, toured their estates, and advocated the adoption of new crop rotations and enlightened husbandry by master and tenant alike. The Woodgates, for instance, promoted the practice of marling (that is, the spreading of clay and lime as a fertiliser) among their tenants; and in 1794, William Woodgate joined George Children in sponsoring the Society for the Encouragement of Agriculture in Kent. In 1800 and 1803, Thomas Mercer of Green Trees, and both William Woodgate and William Francis Woodgate, were closely involved in the opposition to the suspension of duties on hops; they subscribed £20, £20 and £10 respectively, and the latter served on a committee formed to pursue the campaign.

If the extended gentry connection might occasionally be employed on behalf of the agricultural community, to mobilise opinion for or against some proposal which affected its dearest interests, there arose during the Georgian period just as many opportunities for the same mechanism to function on behalf of the wider populace. During the eighteenth century, every scheme to provide better infrastructure amenities required the sanction of a parliamentary statute; and in pursuit of such acts, the influence of the gentry among friendly MPs and government officers, often tilted the balance in the desired direction. Through this procedure, the town and inhabitants of Tonbridge were to benefit from the construction of turnpike roads between Sevenoaks and Pembury and between Tonbridge and Maidstone in 1710 and 1765 respectively. For Georgian Tonbridge, however, the most important of the parliamentary statutes passed during the century was that allowing John Hooker to make the river Medway navigable up to the town. The canalisation of the river had been mooted as early as the reign of Queen Elizabeth, when a group of gentlemen in the area wished to enhance the trade in local iron goods. At that time, the opposition of resident farmers and carters proved insuperable, but in 1740 there were no such difficulties. A series of locks enabled barges to reach the town, where cargoes of hops and timber were loaded and stored at the new Medway wharf and its adjoining warehouses. In an age when government grants and development loans were entirely unknown, a venture like the Medway Navigation Company depended solely upon the enterprise and financial backing of the local gentry. John Hooker raised his capital from the sale of 213 shares at £100 each. A H Neve prints a list of the promoters in

Tonbridge of Yesterday, many of whom went on to become subscribers.[20] Beneath the prestigious titles of the Duke of Dorset and the Earl of Westmorland, are found those of Henry and William Woodgate, Thomas Austen, Sir Thomas Dyke of Hilden, George Hooper, Samuel Mills, and Richard Norris, as well as those of Fraser Honywood, Richard Streatfield, David Polhill, Richard Master of Mereworth, and Sir Thomas Webster. The clergy was also represented, in the persons of the Revd Edmund Latter and the Revd Stephen Cowper; and it is certain that without this breadth of support, the people of Tonbridge would never have reaped the fruits of so transforming a project. By the time Hasted came to pen his survey later in the century, he could describe a 'spacious Wharf, on which a great quantity of the largest oak timber which is brought out of the Wealds of Kent and Sussex, is continually laid, till it can be conveniently wafted down the river to the royal docks at Chatham and Sheerness'.[21] The land tax assessments for 1780 and 1800 also bear testimony to the central position of the Medway Navigation Company in the economic life of the town, with Samuel Mills and his son being responsible for many installations engaged on the river trade.

While acting as the principal source of business capital for provincial expansion, the gentry also owned most of those assets and raw materials increasingly in demand to supply growing national and local populations. Land was a prime commodity, which, as a leading London builder like James Burton of Mabledon knew to his own advantage, might be made to furnish revenues far beyond the perilous limits of agriculture. Towards the end of the eighteenth century, William Woodgate estimated that poor land might yield only five shillings an acre, whereas the fields on the neighbouring Twisden estate could be worth 20 shillings an acre. At about the same time, however, the Blue Barn lands south of the Medway were bought and quickly re-sold at a profit of £3000 by a judicious Maidstone speculator.[22] Parts of the Ferox Hall estate in Bordyke and Hadlow Road were sold for building in the early nineteenth century, and in the 1830s, Mr Alexander of Somerhill released two acres at £100 for the site of the new workhouse, after the Marquis Camden had asked £300 for four acres.

Several other raw materials were at hand for those gentlemen with the means and the foresight to exploit them. In the previous century, there were iron furnaces at Barden and the Postern, and Celia Fiennes writes of 'a great store of oare all over the Country', being used in the casting of guns.[23] During the Georgian period, the ancient iron and textile industries of the Weald were in permanent decline, and for a time, the felling of timber in the South Frith for charcoal production was less vigorous than formerly. However, the advent of the Medway Navigation Company, and Britain's involvement in a series of continental and global wars, made timber once again a precious commodity. The gentry estates of Tonbridge were often found rich in clay, stone, and gravel, so that quarrying frequently offered a valuable addition to the yearly income. The Medway Navigation Company established its own lime kiln, which together with brick-making, gave a fresh impetus to local building activity.

Members of the Tonbridge gentry were not slow to follow John Hooker into the realms of business and commercial enterprise. Hasted speaks of a 'pestle mill' at Old Forge Farm, producing gunpowder after 1763, and in 1772, Thomas Hooker obtained an Act of Parliament for the manufacture of a type of sporting gunpowder known as 'battle gunpowder'.[24] In 1811, the Childrens and the Burtons each ventured £15,000 in another gunpowder scheme at the Ramhurst works in Leigh, which, in its initial phase at least, enjoyed the endorsement of Humphry Davy. Success in business might also be a stepping-stone to a place in the ranks of the gentry. The manufacture of Tunbridge ware, for instance, grew rapidly through the eighteenth century, in a factory in the High Street just north of the Great Bridge. At the height of its fashion, the venture boasted a weekly wage-bill of £38, and a total expenditure of as much as £100; and the land tax returns identify its proprietors, the Wise family, as significant property owners by the end of the century.[25]

Perhaps the most celebrated involvement of the gentry in the commercial life of Georgian Tonbridge is that relating to the establishment of banking. The need for such a facility among the tradesmen is obvious, and it was natural that prominent citizens like George

Children, William Scoones, and the Woodgates should assume the leadership of a concern requiring capital and a great measure of trust. The story of the Tonbridge Bank is well known. Opening its doors in 1792, it flourished long enough for William Francis Woodgate to succeed his father in 1809, only to fail disastrously three years later in a period of acute economic depression, which also numbered one of Jane Austen's brothers among the casualties of a widespread banking hiatus. On the one hand, this episode illustrates clearly the strength of the Georgian gentry, its economic pre-eminence, and its ability to generate and sustain the environment so vital for wealth creation. Yet, on the other hand, it emphasises all the fragility of a social grouping with so narrow a base and strictly limited resources; and, as will be argued later, its costly termination may be seen as coinciding with a general diminution of gentry influence across the whole gamut of Tonbridge affairs.

The gentry and local administration

If economic power was the first pillar of gentry influence in Georgian society, its twin and complementary support was certainly the gentry's monopoly of the offices of local administration. In the eighteenth century, it was widely accepted that the rôle of central government in domestic affairs should not generally extend beyond the maintenance of law and order and the protection of the rights of property. Even in the earliest phases of the Industrial Revolution, parliamentary representation was little more than a reflection of tradition and established privilege, while in the provinces, the larger towns and boroughs remained the jealously-guarded preserve of oligarchic corporations. The principal instrument of administration in the shires was the meeting of Quarter Sessions, held periodically for the Commission of the Peace and the Grand Jury to judge disputes and sentence criminals. On a more day-to-day basis, the justices of the peace upheld the law in their own neighbourhoods, where, for the majority of unincorporated communities, the parish vestry provided the natural forum for deliberation and decision making.

In Tonbridge, the last relics of the ancient feudal administration lingered on throughout the Georgian period, although their vestigial functions had long since slumbered into terminal decay. The direct bonds of service and fealty, forged between the Crown and the holder of demesne lands by the granting of the Medieval Lowy of Tonbridge, had scarcely survived the passing of the Clares and their ilk. Nevertheless, the lord of the manor retained a prestige within the town. His steward continued to sit in judgement over the courts leet and baron, hearing the claims of freeholders, copyholders, and other inhabitants, and dispensing justice in a variety of minor matters. A small amount of patronage also adhered to the manorial dignity. In Hasted's day, for instance, the court leet was responsible for appointing two wardens, whose duties were financed out of a sum of £32, derived from the Town Lands. Other offices, including those of borsholder and hayward, were appointed until 1842.

Many of the administrative powers formerly exercised by the manorial courts had been vested in the Commission of the Peace during the sixteenth century. The justices, who were drawn almost exclusively from the principal gentry and often the Anglican clergy, were charged with the upkeep of roads, with the regulation of prices, wages, and apprenticeships, and with the licensing of ale-houses. They were closely involved in the assessment and collection of the county rates and the land tax, and, as is indicated by the West Malling petty session records from the 1760s, spent by far the greater proportion of their time on business associated with the poor-rates and the investigation of settlement claims.[26] Following the Bridge Act of 1739, the justices found themselves more than ever responsible for the surveying and maintenance of county bridges. Hence, when Tonbridge's Great Bridge was re-built between 1775 and 1776, it fell to Thomas Hooker, Thomas Harvey, and George Children, as the town's justices, to superintend much of the construction, to engage local craftsmen, to arrange for supplies of raw materials, and to administer the £1,104 of county funds made available for the project.[27]

For members of the propertied classes of a town such as Tonbridge, the legal functions of the justices of the peace dovetailed harmoniously with a profound belief in the efficacy of the law. Men like William Scoones owed their enjoyment of wealth and position to the legal profession, which was regarded as a most suitable career for a young Woodgate or Children. The ownership of property meant that few gentlemen were without a well-thumbed legal tome on a convenient shelf, and resort to litigation to settle arguments about land and boundaries frequently appear more as pastimes to be indulged with relish and pursued with dogged resolution. Sitting alone or in pairs, the local justices used petty sessions to deal with cases of larceny, assault, and nuisance, as well as poaching, the theft of animals and clothing, and the sale of underweight or adulterated bread. Malefactors generally received a fine, although short spells of imprisonment, or a public whipping by the parish constable, might be handed down to persistent offenders, with the harshest punishments being reserved for those who transgressed the sanctity of property ownership.

Like the Commission of the Peace, the parish vestry had gradually accumulated a wide sphere of influence over many decades. The parish church, and the priory which once stood south of the Medway, were originally founded as adjuncts to the secular authority of the Norman lords; and in the eighteenth century, no less than in the twelfth century, the ecclesiastical power was associated with the preservation of the status quo. In theory, the parish vestry was open to all parishioners who wished to participate in the running of the town's affairs. In practice, however, meetings attracted little popular interest, with the result that the opinions and preferences of the vicar, churchwardens, and the most influential and articulate inhabitants invariably carried the day. In the estimation of J B Wadmore, the vestry 'practically governed the parish' in the Georgian period.[28] It determined all questions relative to the church and the churchyard, and expended much effort upon the regulation of the workhouse and the countless demands made by the prevailing system of poor relief. In addition to the influence to be derived from the performance of these charitable duties, the vestry possessed the patronage to a number of offices, including those of surveyors of highways, assessors of poor rates, the beadle, and the overseers of the poor. The vestry was also an employer of labour, able to generate work for craftsmen, tradesmen, and builders; and may thus be thought of as a key focus for the many diverse strands of town administration.

Even when the provision of local services passed beyond the direct control of the old parish authorities, there emerged more, rather than fewer, openings for reciprocal patronage. Old Henry Woodgate of Somerhill, for example, served as a turnpike commissioner, and also ranked among the commissioners who were empowered to assess the damage (and hence the levels of compensation) caused while the Medway was being made navigable. The trustees of the Maidstone to Tonbridge turnpike had powers to arrange for the purchase of land for road widening. They required sizeable quantities of building materials such as stone, wood, and iron, as well as much labour to lay down and maintain the road surface, and to collect tolls. Negotiations periodically took place with habitual road users, when preferential rates might be agreed to the advantage of all parties.[29] The eighteenth century cared little about competitive tendering, and was seldom rigorous in its audit of accounts, thereby making it quite natural for justices and trustees to favour craftsmen from their own localities. As office holders within the established administrative mechanisms, the gentry augmented its inherited prestige and tapped deep veins of patronage and vested interest. John Hooker bolstered financial well-being as master of the Medway Navigation Company, with the titular honours of manorial lordship. In like manner, Sir John Dixon Dyke acquired the manor of Hilden in 1763, and in 1767 this same prize passed to the family of Harvey. William Woodgate became a deputy-lieutenant of Kent in 1792, and his eldest son attained to the same office in 1797. George Children and W F Woodgate served as magistrates; the former becoming chairman of the Tonbridge bench, and the latter sitting on the Grand Jury at Maidstone Quarter Sessions. From 1802, both men acted as trustees of the church of King Charles the Martyr in Tunbridge Wells, in company with the Earl Camden and the Earls of Abergavenny and Romney.

Office-holding also offered good prospects of social and economic advancement. In a most illuminating study of the Sevenoaks Austens, Professor Keith-Lucas demonstrates how, between 1753 and 1808, Francis Austen and his son combined the post of Clerk of the Peace for Kent, with a multifarious array of clerkships, secretaryships, and treasurerships to turnpike trusts, the county lieutenancy, and numerous other private estates and municipal foundations, and accumulated thereby, not only considerable wealth, but a degree of influence that ensured for both men, and their connections, a prestige among the gentry and nobility of the Weald.[30]

Within Tonbridge itself, the offices of Town Warden and Church-warden conferred both honour and influence on their custodians.[31] A roll-call of Tonbridge churchwardens in the late eighteenth century records the familiar names of Woodgate, Harvey, Simmons, Eldridge, Dewhurst, Twort, and Mills; and a similar coterie of gentlemen had the management of Town Lands, either in person or through their nominees. The Town Wardens, indeed, were men of considerable stature, since they could appoint to several minor offices, controlled the purchase of local commodities such as gravel and stone, rented meadows to farmers whose lands they adjoined, and regularly employed craftsmen, carters, and labourers. And the gentry was always on hand to lend its weight to special causes. In 1812, for example, George Children, W F Woodgate, and William Scoones were among fifteen 'gentry and tradesmen' elected on to the committee of 'a society to provide a nightly watch to protect property'; while, in September of the following year, the Childrens and the Woodgates were again prominent, on this occasion alongside James Burton, Richard Allnutt, William Wells, Thomas Mercer, and the Tonbridge clergy, in the distribution of bibles among the poor, through the efforts of the Society for the Propagation of Christian Knowledge and local Bible societies.[32]

The privilege of representing the county of Kent in Parliament tended to rest with noble families such as the Sackvilles of Knole, the Marshams of the Mote, and the Fairfaxes of Leeds Castle, or with independent gentry houses like the Derings, the Oxendens, the

Honywoods, and the Knatchbulls, whose pedigrees stretched back into the mists of the Middle Ages. Nevertheless, when county elections came around at about six or seven year intervals, the gentry connections of Tonbridge had an important contribution to make to the overall result. It should perhaps be explained at the outset, that in the eighteenth century the Kent county constituency returned two knights of the shire to sit in the House of Commons. The electorate was composed of the forty-shilling freeholders, each of whom might cast two votes. Candidates often appeared in pairs, usually with one member of the partnership from the western division of the county and one from the eastern division. For much of the century, party labels had a mainly historical and polemical significance, although the 'Whigs' generally favoured the government interest, whereas the 'Tories' tended to proclaim the virtues of independence.

Voting took place on Penenden Heath near Maidstone, and was spread over a number of days, in order to allow freeholders adequate time to make the journey to the polls, where, having listened to the speeches of leading protagonists on either side, each man stood forward to declare his preferences to the returning officer and his clerks. Due to the sheer size and expense of the undertaking, county elections were often uncontested. When a fight was unavoidable, as happened in Kent in 1733, 1754, 1790, 1796, and 1802, the warring parties strove to mobilise every last iota of support. And, on these occasions, the gentry connections, small or large, based upon personal regard, economic dependence, or official necessity, might prove crucial to success or failure.

Two collections of letters among the Sackville manuscripts go far to illuminate the methods adopted during the long weeks of campaigning before the final poll.[33] In 1733 and 1754, the gentry friends of the Duke of Dorset were induced to provide lavish entertainments for neighbouring freeholders, at which it was purposed to extract promises of votes from the feasting throng. Men of business like Francis Austen and Sackville Bale proved invaluable in the organisation of meetings, pamphlets, and broadsheets, and a host of correspondents kept Knole and the Duke in touch with the machinations of the opposition. Clergymen spoke out from their pulpits, and everywhere men were urged to consider how best to exert influence or exploit an interest. Holders of government appointments in the ports, in the post-offices, and along the coast were reminded of their obligations, and promises made about possible future preferments.

A letter among the Woodgate papers describes how electioneering came to Tonbridge in 1802. On 29 June, Mrs Woodgate wrote:

> We are afraid we are going to have a contested election. Honywood's people are canvassing and Mr Polhill was at Tunbridge yesterday and got many votes: and Sir Edward and Mr Hussey called here ten days ago, and went to Mr Children's, the Major's, Lord Boyne's, and Mr Benson's, but said he should not canvass till after the nomination at Maidstone, which is expected very soon. I call his being here and at those places canvassing, don't you? Sir William Geary sent word he should call here this week; I really think it is time they should *begin* if they mean anything.[34]

The intention on these occasions was clearly to woo the principal inhabitants, in the firm belief that more personal and localised factors would bring a phalanx of voters to the hustings in the train of a well-known gentleman.

The printed poll book for 1790 allows an assessment to be made of Tonbridge's freeholder electorate at the end of the eighteenth century. In this election, the candidates were the two sitting members – Filmer Honywood and Lord Romney's son, the Hon. Charles Marsham – and Sir Edward Knatchbull of Mersham Hatch near Ashford. All three men claimed to act independently of party influence, although Knatchbull was known to favour the Prime Minister, William Pitt, and Honywood increasingly inclined towards the Foxite Whigs. Thirty-eight Tonbridge freeholders polled on the first day at Penenden Heath, including Vicesimus Knox of Tonbridge School, William, John, and James Eldridge, John Muggridge, Thomas Mercer, and William West. Thomas Swayne, Henry Austen, Henry Sidney, Thomas Hooker, George and Richard Children, were among the fifty-six to vote on the second day, along with William Simmons of Hadlow, Samuel Mills, William Scoones, John Shirlock, W T Harvey,

Robert Chalklin, William Woodgate, William Dewhurst, and Humphry Steer. A further nine freeholders registered votes on the third day, so that, by the time the polls closed, a total of 103 Tonbridge freeholders had participated in the election, of whom 82 are described as resident in the town and 62 of these as the occupiers of the property carrying the franchise. For the record, the number of votes cast for each candidate was as follows: Honywood 83, Knatchbull 74, and Marsham 49 – a result which broadly reflects the final verdict of the county as a whole.

While the freeholders of Kent decided the outcome of the 1790 election, the direction of French national affairs had already begun to veer dramatically on to that path which would lead ultimately to anarchy, the fall of the Bourbons, and long years of war. Revolution in France lapsed first into terror and then into despotism, while for the people of Britain there arose the dual spectres of sedition at home and invasion from across the Channel. Faced with this crisis, it was natural that the gentry of the kingdom should come forward to shape opinions and organise the forces of resistance, not least in Kent, where the proximity of London radicalism and French grenadiers demanded prompt and decisive measures for self-defence.

During 1792, when the furore over Tom Paine's *Rights of Man* reached its crescendo, the gentry and clergy of Kent participated prominently in the campaign of petitions and loyal addresses to Parliament, and helped in the formation of committees in many Kentish towns, whose declared aim was to correspond with the national Association established by John Reeves. Henry Woodgate of Riverhill was just such an activist; a prosperous lawyer, who, in company with Lord Mansfield, had run the gauntlet of the Gordon rioters back in 1780, and now, perhaps recalling the howl of the desperate mob, strove tirelessly to secure an affirmation of loyalty from the inhabitants of Sevenoaks. By 1794, the object of public attention had shifted to an impending French landing. A county meeting on 8 April approved the Duke of Dorset's plan for the formation of Volunteer corps, and it was resolved that all gentlemen subscribing £10 should serve on a steering committee. The Woodgates of Tonbridge and the Austens of Sevenoaks figure among many squires who helped finance this defensive strategy, and William Francis Woodgate went to the considerable expense of raising and equipping his own corps of yeomanry.[35]

As officers and sponsors of the Volunteers, the gentry re-enacted those same rôles previously identified in parish affairs and at election time. Traditional patterns of leadership and deference persisted, and patronage to commissions and honours inside the corps helped satisfy the ambitions of farmers and freeholders. Even when the initial invasion scare had passed, enthusiastic support for the Volunteer movement continued unabated. Contemporary descriptions abound of colourful, patriotic parades on the lawns of Somerhill and Mote Park, often in the presence of royalty or nobility; while on a more practical level, the Volunteers frequently operated as a militia or police force to quell rural unrest and outbreaks of crime and riot. England survived the French menace; and it did so, not just through the heroism of Nelson and Wellington, but because at county and parish level, the gentry held steady the reins of administration and authority.

The gentry and local amenities

Thus far, the gentry has been viewed in terms of the ownership of property and its ability to influence the governance of Georgian Tonbridge. Bearing in mind the social and political context of the eighteenth century, it is important to stress the positive nature of this contribution. The very considerable improvements in road and river transport, the creation of business enterprises, and the exploitation of local resources, brought great benefits to the town. Faced with the problem of poverty and homelessness, and conscious of the need to enforce the law, the gentry gave extensively of its time and money, in an age without professional civil servants or co-ordinated policing. In other ways, too, the leisure-time activities and philanthropic concerns of the propertied classes bequeathed an enduring legacy to their fellow inhabitants and to succeeding generations of Tonbridge folk.

The historian of the Tonbridge gentry is particularly fortunate to have as a source, the history and collected papers of the Woodgates. The family, and the connection it sustained, was large and diverse; large enough to embrace most of those persons who counted for anything in Georgian Tonbridge, but not so diverse as to prevent regular correspondence and frequent meetings. The numerous letters in the book help to illustrate how the Georgian gentry passed its leisure hours; they reveal, indeed, very personal glimpses of the Woodgates and their friends at play, and do so in a manner whose tone and colour continually recalls the characters and mode of conversation familiar from contemporary literature. Viewed in a wider context, moreover, these insights into the social dimension of gentry life begin to suggest ways in which the tastes and pastimes of a necessarily restricted circle came gradually to influence the thought and conduct of the wider community.

Literature, in a variety of forms, seems to have played an important rôle in the lives of the Woodgates. The young ladies of the family took great delight in the preparation, circulation, and collection of 'charades', 'enigmas', and 'puzzles'; perhaps even, like Emma Woodhouse, preserving the most original in an album for perusal in the great panelled library at Somerhill. Young William Ashburnham evinced some talents as both a poet and a dramatist, and Maria West is said to have produced a novel. Poems, often on a moral or religious theme, passed from cousin to cousin, and it was not uncommon for a local or family event to be celebrated in verse. Several of the Miss Woodgates belonged to a book-club in Tunbridge Wells, and keen anticipation surrounded the arrival of players or an evening of theatricals at Ferox Hall. Evening parties normally encouraged singing and dancing, as well as feasting and cards, while a celebrated London musician was occasionally engaged to enliven an assembly at Somerhill.

The evolution of an educated and articulate gentry, led naturally to a demand for news and information, which, as literacy increased, came to benefit the whole community. The *Maidstone Journal* was founded in 1786 to serve the western division of Kent, and its contents reflect the interests of a leisured and agricultural readership.

Reports of parliamentary debates, foreign dispatches, and Court news appear alongside intelligence from London and Kentish markets. There are notices of auctions and sales of stock, land, and furniture, and offers of employment for journeymen and domestic staff. Proceedings at the Old Bailey and the Maidstone assizes are fully covered, and, while the paper tried hard to preserve a non-partisan stance on politics, it could not but report on elections, county meetings, and the activities of national characters such as Pitt and Charles James Fox. The *Maidstone Journal* regularly published letters and verses contributed by readers; it carried details about the state lottery, and gave notice of forthcoming balls and concerts in Maidstone and Tunbridge Wells. In October 1790, for instance, there appeared an advertisement for Davis' concert in East Malling, where 'Vocal and Instrumental Music', followed by a ball, might be enjoyed at a cost of 2s 6d a ticket.[36] On a day-to-day basis, the gentry called formally and informally upon each other, took tea with each other, and in due season, attended parties to gossip and to make the acquaintance of new neighbours. There were eleven couples in the dance at Green Trees in 1801, and the company partook of 'fish, flesh, fowl and good red herring'. A letter of 1802 describes how Henry Woogate entertained his whole family at Spring Grove, and another of 1824, speaks of 'cards, dancing and musick' at Postern Park, which the twenty-two persons present 'kept up with much spirit until twelve o'clock'. Members of the Volunteer troops attended dinners at Ferox Hall and Somerhill in the 1790s, and the King's birthday celebrations in 1810 attracted Lady Boyne and many others to a splendid ball in Tunbridge Wells, followed by an adjournment, no doubt for toasts and much revelry, to the Kentish Tavern.[37]

While the Tonbridge gentry spent much of its leisure time at home, or in the company of neighbours and relatives, the later Georgian period witnessed a growing penchant for travel. The wealthier families like the Woodgates could afford to maintain a house in London and might, therefore, enjoy all the theatres, exhibitions, concerts, and balls, regularly on offer in the capital at the most fashionable season of the year. The vogue for 'taking the waters' reached its zenith in the heyday of the Prince Regent, luring the nobility, the gentry, and increasingly the better-off professional families, to Tunbridge Wells, Bath, and many other inland spas. The Tonbridge gentry also shared the growing fondness among the well-to-do for holidays at the seaside. Tonbridge stood beside the road to those resorts on the Sussex coast, between Hastings and Worthing, which, as Jane Austen relates in *Sanditon*, became so popular among 'families of thorough gentility and character' in the early nineteenth century. In 1801, a party which included Major Woodgate sampled the fashionable company, plays, and healthy climate at South Bourn, only, in the estimation of Maria Woodgate at least, to find it inferior to Ramsgate. Rose and Sarah Woodgate spent a holiday at Brighton with Mr and Mrs West in 1804; a number of the Woodgate's Humphry connections were at Hastings with a Miss Scoones in 1824; and in 1830 the family of Francis Woodgate of Ferox Hall sojourned at St Leonards 'for the benefit of sea air'. Finally, the most adventurous spirits might even contemplate foreign travel, returning, like the young John George Children, to amaze their neighbours with reminiscences and *objets d'art* from Italy or the Levant.[38]

The hunting and shooting of pheasants and hares was a popular outdoor pastime among the Woodgate gentlemen, while for the ladies, riding was a favourite means of exercise, and the Woodgate sisters at Mountfield took much pride in their flower garden. Among the local events that attracted the family's attention around the turn of the century may be included a wax works at the fair on Leigh green, and a fine show of pictures at Penshurst Place. It was also from about this date that the gentry began to foster and popularise a number of sports. In the summer of 1790 the *Maidstone Journal* reported a bruising prize-fight between Big Ben and Tin Man at Newbury, as well as the race for the King's Plate on the downs outside Canterbury. The gentry of Kent took a special interest in the game of cricket, both as patrons and as players. Subscribers to the *Maidstone Journal* could read about the pioneering fixtures at Mr Lord's ground, and follow the fortunes of matches such as that made between Kent and the combined strength of Surrey and Hampshire by the Duke of Dorset, which was played at the Vine ground in Sevenoaks for a purse of one thousand guineas.[39] The Woodgates were evidently enthusiastic cricketers. Their correspondence contains references to a game between Somerhill and the Postern, to 'a grand match of cricket' between the Postern club and Peckham in 1800, and to a contest at Leigh in 1802 between Tonbridge and Wrotham.[40]

Though frequently engaged in the pursuit of business or pleasure, it is remarkable how many of the Tonbridge gentry retained an awareness of the virtues of charity, civic pride, and personal edification. Special collections and gifts of food and clothing were often organised privately or through the church, to supplement the resources of the poor-rates at times of acute dearth. Early in 1812, for instance, an 'extremely numerous' audience, 'composed of the most respectable families in the neighbourhood', attended a concert at the Court Hall in Tonbridge, held 'for the benefit of the Poor'. 'The instrumental part was performed by the Gentlemen of the Tunbridge Band. – The vocal part by the Choristers of Tunbridge Church, who very handsomely volunteered their services on the occasion'; and, as the *Maidstone Journal* reported with satisfaction, the evening yielded a 'net profit' of £40, 'to be distributed in meat and bread among the necessitous families in the parish'.[41]

Bequests in the wills of well-to-do men and women provided a more permanent source of relief. Thomas Deakins bequeathed £50 in 1707 for the building of alms-houses, and the will of George Petley set aside £200 for a similar purpose. In Hasted's day, John Hooker of Brenchley (a cousin of the Tonbridge Hookers) was responsible for the administration of John Petley's 1705 gift of money to buy wheaten loaves for the poor. Funds were set aside, by Deakins and others, to provide apprenticeships, while Strong's charity and the 1750 will of Sir John Dixon Dyke of Hilden, sought to ensure a basic education for local children.[42] In 1798, William Woodgate financed the building of the Old Town Hall just north of the Great Bridge, while in the will of his uncle, Henry Woodgate, the sum of £600 was set aside for the provision of a new church organ. George Hooper gave £500 in 1759 to 'new pew and pave' the church, and in 1821,

John Luxford of Ferox Hall made a gift of land in Bordyke to permit the extension of the burial ground.

Perhaps the most enduring of the Tonbridge benefactions was the foundation of a Free Grammar school by Sir Andrew Judde in the reign of Edward VI. By the Georgian period, the original bequest had been augmented by other endowments, notably that of Sir Thomas Smith, so that various scholarships and exhibitions to the Universities were available to the pupils. Long decades of decline were followed by a dispute over the right of inhabitants to an education under the foundation, which was not settled until the 1760s. From that date, children who 'could write competently, and read Latin and English perfectly', should be instructed 'on proper application to the master, without payment of any consideration excepting the statutable entrance-money'.[43] The school continued to open its doors to a surprising cross-section of townsfolk in the decades immediately following this judgement; but thereafter it existed more and more 'to afford to the gentry, the clergy, the liberal professions, and in particular, the middle ranks of society, the means and advantages of an education at once pious, solid and comprehensive'.[44]

Many of the leading Tonbridge families of the eighteenth century can be found represented among the forty to sixty boys constantly on the school roll. George Children and John George Children were both educated at the school, as were several generations of Woodgates, down to the sons of Major Woodgate in the early 1800s. Progression to the Universities then stood open to those desirous of pursuing a clerical career. Francis Woodgate, one of the younger sons of John Woodgate, and the future incumbent of Mountfield, went up to Trinity College, Oxford, on a Smythe exhibition in 1727,[45] and George Austen prepared himself for the family living at Steventon within the walls of St John's. The shared experiences of youth and education did much to foster that commonality of intellectual and cultural values which so characterised and strengthened the Georgian gentry, as did also the practice of employing former pupils like Thomas Roots and George Austen as masters and ushers.[46]

The links of friendship and trust formed at school might serve as potent connections in later life. Such distinguished alumni as Admiral Sir William Sidney Smith, Archbishop Alexander, the Earl of Pembroke and Lord Maletworth of Knole, and John Woodfall, the newspaper editor and champion of parliamentary reporting, all acquired high reputations in public affairs, and in consequence, could be called upon to render advice and assistance, or to provide an introduction. The benign patronage of the Earl of Pembroke, for example, sustained a man of humble origins like Thomas Roots in his post as Master between 1668 and 1714, and later smoothed the way to ecclesiastical preferment for Roots' sons.

Backed by the resources of the London Skinners Company, and possessed of considerable patronage, the Master and ushers of Tonbridge School remained influential figures throughout the Georgian era. It was customary for alms to be distributed on Founder's Day, and a benevolent attitude persisted towards the education and succour of the town's poor throughout the period. Regular purchases of food and fuel brought business to local tradesmen, boarders often lodged in the town, and projects such as the building of a new library benefited students and craftsmen alike. The Tonbridge Fellowship at St John's College, Oxford, was among the prizes in the gift of the Master, vicar and other leading townsmen, and among those to benefit in this period were members of the Mills, Woodgate, West, and Knox families.[47] All the masters were scholars who published on classical and literary themes; James Cawthorn, for instance, was celebrated as a minor poet, and gained popularity as a convivial host, especially at the annual visitation. The Knox family provided three generations of masters between 1771 and 1843, binding still closer the interests of town and gown. The Vicesimus Knoxes, father and son, maintained the ties with St John's College in Oxford, the latter, who married the daughter of a local tradesman, being particularly noted as a writer and preacher. Dr Thomas Knox, Master from 1812 until 1843, served also as curate of Tonbridge, and married the daughter of William Francis Woodgate. The school flourished under the rule of the Knox dynasty, and came to symbolise the confidence and unity of the gentry and propertied classes in Georgian Tonbridge.

Conclusion: the gentry steps aside

As the Georgian age reached its conclusion in the early decades of the nineteenth century, a host of new and radical forces had already begun their work of irreversible change. The pivotal rôle of the gentry in eighteenth-century society is undoubted; yet, to analyse the reasons under-pinning the success and influence of these propertied and landed classes, is, at the same time, to reveal the causes of their inevitable decline.

The family connection and the judicious exploitation of patronage were potent tools when employed in a narrow, close-knit, and deferential provincial community. But, in the early decades of the nineteenth century, more and more of the old Tonbridge estates found themselves in the hands of outsiders; wealthy London builders and bankers like James Burton at Mabledon and James Alexander at Somerhill, or a Lincolnshireman such as William Bailey at the Castle, who had scant understanding of their adopted town, and perhaps no immediate rapport with its inhabitants. The rapid growth and increased mobility of the population after 1800, dealt another fatal blow at the ethos of such a social structure. Likewise, the economic problems which provoked a slump in agriculture towards the end of the Napoleonic Wars, only hastened the migration of people from the countryside to the urban centres. Old allegiances and old loyalties counted for little in the sprawling towns, where wage-earning and the uncertainties of the labour market severely weakened the traditional relationships between landlord and tenant and between master and man.

The establishment of new parishes in Tunbridge Wells, Southborough, Hildenborough, and within Tonbridge itself from the late 1820s onwards, reflects a belated attempt by the old order to satisfy the needs of a new age. But with urbanisation came the problems of crime, poverty, and public health. The hard-pressed justices were ill-equipped to cope with an explosion of theft and pick-pocketing, lacking either the knowledge or the resources to prevent or detect malefactors. The support accorded to schemes for a 'nightly watch or patrole' in the early nineteenth century, is indicative, both of mounting dismay among property owners and of a widespread acknowledgement that established institutions were powerless to cope.[48] The strain upon the poor-rates became intolerable in times of depression, and it was everywhere necessary to re-introduce the wasteful distribution of outdoor relief. Epidemics of cholera might strike almost without warning in the crowded, insanitary courts beside the river, raising a chorus of complaints and demands for immediate remedy.

As the nineteenth century gathered pace, the vestry and the old poor law mechanisms proved unequal to the tasks confronting them. The Poor Law Amendment Act of 1834 re-established the workhouse system on a sounder and wider basis, and a series of sanitation committees and boards gradually assumed responsibility for other urban improvements, until the Tonbridge Local Board took sole charge in 1870. On these bodies, amateur administrators, drawn from the gentry and clergy, were no substitute for Edwin Chadwick's new breed of skilled professionals. Public attitudes towards office-holding and accountability were also evolving rapidly. Notions of democracy and utility gained steadily in popularity, making patronage and personal interest far less tolerable, and inevitably weakening the influence of individuals and narrow oligarchies.

The influence of the Anglican church, for so long a source of stability in provincial communities, was similarly waning as the new era opened. The collection of tithes bred a festering resentment against the clergy, as did the imposition of church-rates on nonconformists, and the apparently reactionary and venal predilections of the bench of bishops. The first congregation of Protestant dissenters was established in Tonbridge in 1751, and the preaching of Wesley and other Methodists often proved more attractive to urban ears. Neither could the church's monopoly in the provision of education as a charitable office be expected to cater for new and varied urban and professional needs. The charity school of Hasted's day gave place to the first National School in 1818, just as the limitations of the classical curriculum available under the Tonbridge School foundation gradually spawned a host of private academies like that of the Revd Mr Jefferson in the 1790s.[49]

There is no real evidence that national affairs or politics aroused any great passions in Tonbridge during the eighteenth century. Only the gentry and substantial freeholders could participate in county elections, and when contests did occur, the rivalry turned more on personality than on particular issues. Events like the Gordon Riots of 1780, and the progress of the French Wars and the Volunteers, did excite brief mention in the correspondence of the Woodgates; but even here, references are thinly scattered, and quickly give place to more personal and domestic subjects. The spread of literacy and the dramatic growth of the national and provincial press helped dispel this introspection. The Kentish Gazette and the Maidstone Journal devoted more and more space to the events of the day, publishing letters and addresses, reporting county and borough meetings, and adopting distinctive attitudes on controversial topics. In this way, public consciousness was formed and directed on such matters as social reform, Catholic Emancipation, and, most spectacularly, on the movement for parliamentary reform after 1830. Dr Thomas Knox was an outspoken advocate of a wider franchise, making his views public at Penenden Heath, and organising a celebration at Tonbridge School when the Reform Bill triumphed in June 1832.

Finally, in the sphere of economics and commerce, where John Hooker and his gentry backers had so benefited the Tonbridge of 1740, the weaknesses of the passing order were plain for all to observe. The gentry could never hope to supply even a modest business like the Medway Navigation Company with sufficient capital to expand and remain competitive. The constant resort to litigation is a clear indication of insecurity and an inability to respond to new challenges from rivals like James Christie. As a result, through much of its later history, the company suffered from inefficiency and unprofessional management, and the parlous state of its towpaths, locks, and bridges testified to neglect and chronic under-funding. The collapse of the Tonbridge Bank in 1812, and the similar fate suffered by a second venture launched by Thomas Mercer and John Barlow in 1813, also serve to underline the limitations of the gentry as financiers and entrepreneurs. Gentlemen might once have established turnpikes and built locks on the river, but the complexities of banking, never mind the construction of a railway, demanded far greater resources, coupled with the sort of expertise offered to the Victorians by a Thomas Beeching.

The bankruptcy of George Children and William Francis Woodgate in 1816 was a great personal tragedy; it also somehow symbolises the passing of a whole way of life from the Tonbridge scene. Somerhill and Ferox Hall remained, but the gentry, as arbiters of Tonbridge fortunes, had effectively stepped aside. The funeral of George Children, who had died in exile in 1818, roused the people of Tonbridge to mourn the loss of a respected neighbour, benefactor, and eminent man of property. His career had epitomised everything that bound the gentry so tightly into its local community. Born and raised locally, and educated in the town among his peers, Children strove throughout a busy life to uphold the laws and customs of his society, to alleviate the harsher extremities of his age, and to advance the prosperity of Tonbridge wherever possible. Though fated at last to fall from grace, he did so without sacrificing his dignity or his good name, retiring, rather, into a quiet backwater to allow new men and different ideals to assume the cares of leadership. Hence, when Francis Woodgate of Riverhill bought Ferox Hall in 1820, it was quite impossible that any gentleman, no matter how wealthy or well-connected, could ever again enjoy the influence once accorded to his uncle or to the former master of his newly-acquired home.

Sources

Principal manuscript and printed sources are listed here. Specific references are cited in the notes, but no attempt has been made to supply a comprehensive guide to the many books which contain information about Tonbridge and its gentry.

Manuscript sources
Centre for Kentish Studies: Land Tax Assessments for Tonbridge Town, 1780
and 1800; the Sackville manuscripts
Newspapers
The Maidstone Journal

Printed sources
Defoe, D, *A Tour through the Whole Island of Great Britain*, ed. P Rogers
(London,1971)
Fiennes, C, *The Illustrated Journeys of Celia Fiennes 1685 – c.1712*, ed. C Morris
(London,1982)
Finch, *Directory of Kent* (1803)
Hasted, E, *The History and Topographical Survey of the County of Kent ...*, second
edition, 12 vols. (Canterbury,1798)
Neve, A H, *The Tonbridge of Yesterday* (Tonbridge,1933)
Seymour, C, *A New Historical, Topographical, and Commercial Survey of the
Cities, Towns and Villages of the County of Kent* (Canterbury,1776)
Wadmore, B, *Some Details on the History of the Parish of Tonbridge*
(Tonbridge,1906)
Woodgate, G and G M G, *A History of the Woodgates of Stonewall Park and of
Summerhill in Kent, and their Connections* (printed for private circulation, Wisbech,
[1910])

Notes

1   Ireland, S W H, *England's Topographer; or A New and Complete History of
    the County of Kent, from the Earliest Records to the Present Time*, 4 vols.
    (London, 1828-30), iii, p359
2   Mingay, G E, *English Landed Society in the Eighteenth Century*
    (London,1963), p3
3   Chalklin, C W, 'A Seventeenth-century Market Town: Tonbridge' in
    M Roake and J Whyman, *Essays in Kentish History* (London,1973)
4   Chalklin, C W, 'A Kentish Wealden Parish (Tonbridge) 1550-1750'
    (B.Litt. thesis, Oxford University,1960), pp130-134
5   Hasted, vol. V, p200
6   Fiennes, p125
7   Defoe, pp141-149
8   Seymour, p778
9   Seymour, pp776-777

10 Mingay, *English Landed Society in the Eighteenth Century*, p23
11 Woodgate and Woodgate, pp371-373
12 Namier, Sir L B, *The Structure of Politics at the Accession of George III* (sec. edition, London,1957)
13 Mingay, *English Landed Society in the Eighteenth Century*, p3
14 Hasted, vol. V, p197
15 Woodgate and Woodgate, ch. iii, xiv, and xvii
16 Woodgate and Woodgate, pp56 and 449. Cf 'Knole House and the Home Farm 1716-1739': collection of essays by pupils of Tonbridge School
17 Hasted, vol. V, p197
18 Woodgate and Woodgate, pp351-352
19 Woodgate and Woodgate, pp319 and 320-22
20 Neve, p19
21 Hasted, vol. V, p198
22 Neve, p44
23 Fiennes, p128
24 Hasted, vol. V, p197
25 Wadmore, ch 8
26 'A Petty Sessions in the Eighteenth Century': collection of essays by pupils of Tonbridge School
27 Chalklin, C W, 'Bridge Building in Kent, 1700-1830: The Work of the Justices of the Peace' in A Detsicas and N Yates, *Studies in Modern Kentish History Presented to Felix Hull and Elizabeth Melling* ... (Maidstone,1983) pp49-63
28 Wadmore, p66
29 'The Finances of a Turnpike Company': collection of essays by pupils of Tonbridge School
30 Keith-Lucas, B, 'Francis and Francis Motley Austen, Clerks of the Peace for Kent' in A Detsicas and N Yates, *Studies in Modern Kentish History Presented to Felix Hull and Elizabeth Melling* ... (Maidstone,1983) pp87-102
31 Wadmore, pp17-23, contains list of churchwardens
32 *Maidstone Journal*, 11 February 1812, 7 and 28 September 1813
33 Letters to the Duke of Dorset in the Sackville MSS
34 Woodgate and Woodgate, pp368-69
35 Humphries, P L, 'Kentish Politics and Public Opinion 1768-1832' (D.Phil. thesis, Oxford University, 1981), pp162-69
36 *Maidstone Journal*, 12 October 1790
37 Woodgate and Woodgate, pp306, 358, 430, 223, 431

38 Woodgate and Woodgate, pp364, 305, 222, 284
39 *Maidstone Journal*, 7 September and 20 July 1790
40 Woodgate and Woodgate, pp362, 53, 368
41 *Maidstone Journal*, 4 February 1812
42 Hasted, vol. V, pp248-50
43 Hasted, vol. V, pp243-44
44 *A Concise History of Tonbridge School* (London,1827), p5
45 Woodgate and Woodgate, p45
46 Hoole, G P, *A Tonbridge Miscellany* (Canterbury,1985), pp20-32
47 Wadmore, pp47-48, on the Tonbridge Fellowship
48 *Maidstone Journal*, 28 January and 11 February 1812
49 *Maidstone Journal*, 20 July 1790

Mabledon and its Owners 1803–1830

Gwenyth Hodge

About half-a-mile south of Tonbridge Station lies Quarry Hill, rising to approximately 360 feet above sea-level. The name derives from a quarry which until recent years lay on the left-hand side of the road leading from Tonbridge to Tunbridge Wells. This is no longer obvious, as the construction in 1971 of the Tonbridge bypass flyover which today carries the A26 over the A21 completely altered the area.[1]

On the west side of Quarry Hill, just south of the flyover, lies Mabledon, which was built by James Burton in 1804, and stone from the quarry may well have been used in the building of the house. (Approximately 22 acres of the estate were affected by the 1971 road works.)

James Haliburton was born on 29 July 1761, and was baptised in the Presbyterian Chapel, Soho. He came of a Roxburghshire family and was educated in London. In June 1776 he was placed with Mr Dalton, Surveyor, and articled on the 29th July following for six years. At the expiration of his articles he entered into partnership with Mr Dalton.

On 1 March 1783 James married Miss Elizabeth Westley at St Clement Danes and the couple had twelve children. The first four were baptised under the name of Haliburton, but for some obscure reason involving a family disagreement James Haliburton changed his name to the shortened 'Burton'. The fourth child, James, a distinguished archaeologist, returned to the name of Haliburton in 1838 – the only one to do so.

James Burton left a small leather-covered notebook which gives some details of both his private life and his professional activities.[2]

That he was a most successful business man is obvious from the fact that in 1786, immediately before his father's death, his assets were £1,404, and by 1789 they had risen to £12,505. Burton was the biggest London builder of his time, and he recorded that in the year 1800 he made 8,140,000 bricks and in 1801, 10,368,000.

Between 1798 and 1803 James Burton developed a large part of the Bloomsbury Estate in London for the Duke of Bedford, and the present Headquarters of the British Medical Association in Tavistock Square stands on the site of Burton's back garden. Burton's connection with the region is perpetuated by certain street names in the Euston area: Tonbridge Street, Judd Street, Bidborough Street and Mabledon Place.

Burton's building activities for the period 1785 to 1823 were summarised in a paper found by his son, Alfred, after his death. It shows that in that period Burton erected estates comprising 2,366 buildings in and around London to a total value of £1,848,900. (Twenty-seven of these buildings were in Kent. The figures exclude buildings erected for others under Burton's superintendence.)

It was in the early years of the nineteenth century that James Burton developed an interest in the Tonbridge area. J Manwaring Baines, in *Burton's St.Leonards*, records that in December 1803, while 'riding his pony to Penshurst, Burton was very nearly drowned in a flood.' In 1804 he purchased some land which had originally been part of South Frith Estate – a great Norman hunting chase and one of the divisions of the demesne of Tonbridge dating from the Middle Ages.

In the sixteenth century the forest was being cleared gradually, and one or two farms appeared, though part of the land remained rough until quite a late date.

Towards the close of the seventeenth century the owner was John, Earl of Buckingham (self-styled), and a Quadripartite Indenture dated 10 December 1702, exists between John, Earl of Buckingham, Henry Weller, Gent. of Sussex, Christopher Eldridge, Yeoman of Tonbridge, and John Amrock of Fletching in Sussex. Under this Christopher Eldridge is recorded as acquiring:

... one barn standing near the top of Quarry Hill in Tonbridge and four pieces or parcles [sic] of land containing by estimation fourteen acres lying near unto the said barn; and also nine several pieces or parcels of land containing by estimation twenty acres bounding to the highway ...

From the mention of 'the top of Quarry Hill' and lands 'bounding to the highway' it is probable that this was the land on which Mabledon was eventually built. Christopher Eldridge I left the land to his son, Christopher Eldridge II (1701-99). Thence it descended to his nephew, the Revd Thomas Baker, perpetual curate of Chiddingstone, who sold it to James Burton for £6,250. Thomas Baker had leased the land for a period of 21 years to Hannah Pocock, widow of Thomas Pocock, the lease commencing on 10 October 1784. When the lease ran out in 1805 it appears that James Burton purchased the property and built himself a new house, designed by the architect Joseph T Parkinson, being one of his earliest important commissions.

In an abstract of a title deed the earlier property is described as 'that messuage or tenement and farm with the appurtenances called Mapleton alias Measells alias Godfreys or by whatsoever name or names the same were or had been called or known'. In the Tithe Map of 1838 the spelling is Mableton.

Paul Amsinck in *Tunbridge Wells and its neighbourhood*, published in 1810, provides an interesting account of the new house:

... In fixing upon the style of Mabledon, it was very probably thought that neither the neatness, or rather spruceness of the Italian nor the elaborate elegance of the Grecian architecture, would harmonise with the bold character of the grounds. It was therefore determined to adopt the castellated form with a mixture of the Gothic. But however antique the exterior appearance may be, the interior is of the most modern description. The apartments are of good dimensions; and are so disposed that each of the principal rooms looks upon a different prospect. The stone, of which the house is built, was dug upon the premises; having the property of hardening by exposure; and is of a remarkably durable quality ...

In July 1804, James Burton moved with his family to Quarry Hill, naming the estate Mabledon Park, and 'engaged a bailiff and game-keeper at 40 guineas a year'. He was interested in genealogy and the small notebook, already mentioned, contains some details of his family and personal notes, but this ended in 1811.

The notebook reveals him as an active and adventurous man, loving in his care for all members of his family whether closely related or not, proud of his possessions and scrupulously careful in his accounts.

Quite soon after his move to Tonbridge he began to lead a more social life: in 1809 he and Mrs Burton dined with the Lord Mayor at the Guildhall, and in the following year he was pricked for High Sheriff of Kent and sworn in on 14 February 1810. He was an active JP in the county, attending the Quarter Sessions meeting at Maidstone on 7 April 1812, which received the report of the architect, Daniel Alexander, on the first year of building the county gaol.

James Burton's family of six girls and six boys were all born before his move to Mabledon. There are references to the family in *The History of the Woodgates of Stonewall Park and of Summerhill, Kent,* and it is evident that they quickly entered into the social life of the Tonbridge area. They entertained themselves and attended parties elsewhere as at Somerhill.

After settling into his new house and giving attention to the laying-out of the grounds, James Burton attended to the road from Tonbridge to Tunbridge Wells which passed close by his property. It is known that when the Woodgates of Summerhill went visiting in the seventeenth century they took with them piles of stakes to repair the road, and although the introduction of the turnpike system had brought some improvement the condition of the roads in general still left much to be desired.[3]

The scheme, financed largely by Burton himself, entailed the cutting of a completely new stretch of road through the hill which, as well as easing the gradient, took the road to the Wells further away from his house. Other local activities included building a house for a son at Barden in the valley nearer Tonbridge town in 1809-10. Under the pressure of growing demand during the Napoleonic Wars

Mabledon, from Amsinck's *Tunbridge Wells and its neighbourhood*, 1810.
(Source: Tonbridge Reference Library)

James and this son, William Ford, were partners in setting up a gunpowder works at Ramhurst Mills in the adjoining parish of Leigh in 1811, contributing £15,000 out of £30,000 capital. The whole of the works was bought by W F Burton in 1820 and remained in the family's hands until 1859. James participated like other local notables in good works.

Although the main concern of this paper is with the Mabledon estate and its owners, as part of the development of Tonbridge, it is nevertheless interesting to note that round about the year 1827 James Burton, with a successful career behind him, set out to found a new town of his own, St Leonards, near Hastings. This final venture was not exactly welcomed by his sons. Nevertheless the family went down to St Leonards and several of them lived there.

Baines records that, 'Not content with building houses, it was typical of the man that he should endeavour to improve the lot of those who might live in them'. In December 1831 he issued 'Cottage

Regulations recommended for the Preservation of Health', including such suggestions as regular washing of floors, opening of windows, removal of refuse and even personal items of clothing and diet, including abstention from 'indulgence in spirituous liquors'. Burton is the undisputed founder of St. Leonards, where he and his wife are buried. A memorial tablet in the Church there records that he died on 31 March 1837 – little more than two months after the death of his wife.

Although James Burton was rightly renowned as a builder, his son, Decimus – who was four years old when the move to Tonbridge took place – was to achieve considerably more fame as an architect. He benefited from his father's reputation and his training with John Nash. His notable buildings included the Athenaeum Club and two imposing villas in the Inner Circle area of Regent's Park. Other important commissions followed: in 1827, as a comparatively young man, he was entrusted with the laying-out of the Zoological Gardens, and later with the well-known entrance gateway to Hyde Park Corner. Decimus Burton was responsible for the erection of the Conservatory at Chatsworth – the largest conservatory then built – which had a cast-iron frame.

Decimus Burton's name is inextricably linked with that of Richard Turner, an ironfounder, in the building in 1844-48 of the Great Palm House in the Royal Botanic Gardens at Kew – which has recently been restored. Its construction was based on the latest techniques in ship-building.[4] More local examples of his work include the Calverley Estate and Holy Trinity Church (1828-29) in Tunbridge Wells.[5] The planning of the picturesque Calverley Estate in 1828 was influenced by Nash's work in Regent's Park. Decimus built a house for himself and three houses in Calverley Parade, all now demolished. He also altered Mabledon for a new owner, John Deacon (1829-31). Another of James Burton's sons, also James, took an early interest in geology and became a distinguished Egyptologist.

James Burton sold Mabledon in 1817 to N Sturt. He passed it to Sir Anthony Hart KC in 1818 or 1819, who occupied it for about ten years.

Hart was the youngest son of William and Sarah Hart. He was born on 17 April 1757 on the island of St Christopher, and was a pupil at Tonbridge School from 1765 to 1770(?). He had a brilliant career, being admitted to the Middle Temple on 22 January 1776, and called to the Bar on 29 June 1781. He practised in the Court of Chancery, becoming a KC in 1807 and a Bencher in the same year. In addition, he was appointed Solicitor-General to Queen Charlotte in 1813.

Hart appeared as leading Counsel for Tonbridge School in pro-tracted and complex litigation, which continued from 1820 to 1827, concerning School property in London and the precise meaning of Sir Andrew Judd's will. As a result the School's finances were trans-formed. In the Biographical Notes contained in *The Register of Tonbridge School from 1553 to 1820* it is stated as 'a fact without precedent that not a single decision of his was ever varied or reversed'.[6] He was described as 'An amiable man, a sound lawyer and a patient and urbane judge'.

In 1827 he was appointed Vice Chancellor and in the same year was admitted to the Privy Council and knighted. From 1827 to 1830 he was Lord Chancellor of Ireland.

Anthony Hart married Martha Jefferson, who died on 8 May 1819. He himself died on 6 December 1831, in Cumberland Street, London, leaving one daughter, Elizabeth Martha, who married the Revd John Humphry Davis.

Mabledon had been purchased in 1828 by John Deacon I, a successful banker.

In the eighteenth and nineteenth centuries a large number of banks were in existence, and over the years many mergers and take-overs took place, resulting in frequent changes of name. One such – Williams Deacon's Bank – which ended its separate existence in 1970 when its business was merged in a larger institution, Williams & Glyn's Bank Ltd., had itself taken over in 1890 Williams Deacon & Co. of Birchin Lane, London, which had been founded in 1771.

It was in 1826 that John Deacon I, then aged 54, had joined Williams Deacon & Co., having a few years previously retired from a partnership in Baring Bros. & Co.

The preface to a volume entitled *Williams Deacon's 1771-1970*, published in 1970 states: 'In the present volume it is the two hundred years since 1771 in the saga of Williams Deacon's which are being covered and these pages contain something of the history of the individual banks and of the interesting personalities who have been connected with them.' John Deacon I, with whom we are concerned as the owner of Mabledon, is one such interesting personality.

It was in December 1825 that a severe banking crisis arose, in the course of which a number of banks came to grief. A very full account of the crisis and the various moves taken by some of the families in an effort to rescue something from the crash appears in letters published in *Williams Deacon's 1771-1970* (pages 71- 86). Writing from Battersea Rise on January 1st or 2nd 1826, to her aunt, Mrs Hannah More, Miss Marianne Thornton (daughter of the famous banker and philanthropist, Henry Thornton) gave a lively account of the crisis, one paragraph of which is relevant to our subject. She wrote:

> Among the last resources somebody mentioned our neighbour at Broomfield, Mr Deacon, late Partner of the Barings, who made £19,000 a year, and retired from business some years – and it was thought he might know of some one ... so when we met at breakfast, a disconsolate, pale faced lot things already looked better ... Mr Williams had routed out Deacon, who to our amaze confessed that time had been very heavy on his hands ever since he had quitted business – that he had a large family growing up, he had a regard for Henry, and in short that he thought he should like it. They gave him 24 hours, by which time he consented if the accounts proved as satisfactory as was stated. He and Henry have rummaged over them like two cats after mice, and being thoroughly satisfied, it was yesterday settled that young Williams, Deacon and Henry and John Melville, whom Henry has brought in, start on Monday – and the young Baring who is now in Hope's House in Amsterdam comes in after a few weeks.

In addition to being a successful banker, John Deacon was an active Churchman of strong Evangelical principles, and after his arrival at Mabledon quickly took a lively interest in the Church life of the area. Recognising the need for a Church to serve the population which was growing up mid-way between Tonbridge and Tunbridge Wells, he obtained the consent of Sir Charles Hardinge, the Vicar of Tonbridge, to his plan to build a church on Southborough Common, and once again the architect employed was Decimus Burton. A relatively small church, St Peter's, designed to seat approximately 750 worshippers, was erected by subscription at a cost of approximately £4,000 and consecrated on 25 August 1830. The major contributions came from John Deacon and Broadley Wilson of Southborough, and an elaborate memorial to the latter appears high up on the South wall.

An admission ticket for the Consecration survives in the Centre for Kentish Studies Office, and shows that traffic jams are obviously not a new problem: the ticket includes an interesting instruction, 'Carriages to set down with their horses' heads towards Tunbridge Wells.'

The church became the church of the Deacon family and the family vault is in the churchyard.

In quite a short time Mabledon was owned by three outstanding professional men – a builder, a lawyer and a banker. the sons of its builder had also begun different careers by 1830. All the owners derived their wealth from London. In separate ways they made an important contribution to the history of the parish in the early nineteenth century.

Sources

Amsinck, P, *Tunbridge Wells and its neighbourhood*, illustrated by a series of etchings, and historical descriptions (London, 1810)

Baines, J M, *Burton's St. Leonards* (Hastings Museum, 1956)

Chalklin, C W (ed), *New Maidstone Gaol Order Book, 1805-1823*. (Kent Records 23, Maidstone, 1984)

Colvin, H M, *A Biographical Dictionary of British Architects, 1600-1840* (London, 1978)

Hart, W G, *The Register of Tonbridge School from 1553 to 1820 with a list of Head Masters and Ushers and an introduction* (Rivingtons, London, 1935).

Melling, E (ed), *Kentish Sources III: Aspects of Agriculture and Industry* (Maidstone, 1961)

Minter, S, *The greatest glass house: the rainforests recreated* (Royal Botanic Gardens, Kew/HMSO, 1990)

Moule, The Revd A W H, *A History of Mabledon, Tonbridge* (1971)

Orchard, H B, *A look at the Head and the Fifty: a history of Tonbridge School.* (James & James, 1991)

Pownall, T, Manuscript, Mabledon (1975)

Rivington, S, *The History of Tonbridge School,* second edition (London,1898)

Williams Deacon's Bank Ltd, *Williams Deacon's, 1771-1970,* (Manchester, 1971)

Woodgate,The Revd G W and G M G, *A History of the Woodgates of Stonewall Park and of Summerhill in Kent, and their Connections* (printed for private circulation, Wisbech, [1910])

Notes

1   Tonbridge bypass was opened on 12th July 1971 by the then Prime Minister, the Rt Hon Edward Heath.

2   Considerable information on James Burton's business activities is given in Baines.

3   The road from Tonbridge to Pembury was the first in Kent to be turnpiked.

4   For a detailed description of the part played by Decimus Burton in the building of the great Palm House at Kew see Minter.

5   Now Trinity Arts Centre.

6   See Hart.

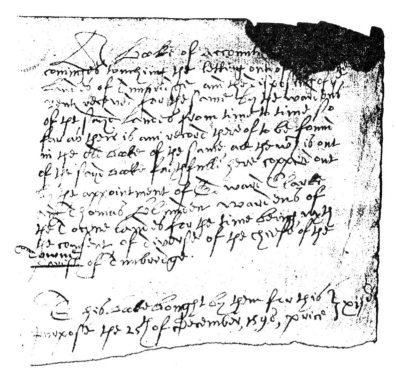

The first entry in the oldest surviving Town Wardens' account book.

'The Booke of Accountes and [blot] cominges touching the letting out of the Towne Landes of Tunbridge and the disposing of ye rents receved for the same by the Wardens of the sayd Landes from time to time so far as there is ani record thereof to be found in the old booke of the same, all of wch is out of the sayd booke faythfulli here coppied out by the appointment of Edward Clarke and Thomas Blunden Wardens of the Town Landes for the time being wyth the consent of diverse of the chiefs of the ["Parish" deleted and in another hand overwritten at a later date] Towne of Tunbredge.

This booke bought by them for this   )
purpose the 25th December, 1598, price) xii d'

82

The Work of the Town Wardens

Sydney Simmons

Introduction

For over four hundred years the Town Wardens kept records of how they let the Town Lands and spent the profits. This story of their work in Georgian times is based on the documents which survive and on notes kept by one Warden.

The Charity

The Wardens of the Town Lands of Tonbridge are Trustees of a Charity which was in existence before 1571 and legally registered in an Indenture of 1575 dealing with 'eight parcels of Land and Meadow commonly called the Town Lands containing in the whole by estimation thirty acres more or less'. The Indenture names eight Wardens, who, when reduced to five by death, were to make up their numbers to eight, and so on for ever. Their duties were to let the lands to the best advantage and with the profits:

> to sustain and maintain or newly to re-edify all the Bridges in the Town of Tonbridge (excepting the Great Bridge which the Lord of the Town is in right to maintain), ... and if there be any surplusage over and above the needful reparations of the said Bridges then the same to be employed for the amending of the ways within the said Town.

The first mention of The Town Lands is in a document of 1431 dealing with a land transaction near Lodge Oak. During a dispute which ran from 1628 to 1637 evidence was given connecting the Indenture with the discovery of an intent by some Wardens to sell away the Town Lands for their own ends. The outcome of the dispute was a legal Decree which established that there were to be two Wardens who were to be elected by the townsmen for a three year term at Michaelmas; they were to enter into bonds with the Surveyors to let the Town Lands for unspecified periods, and any profits left after they had maintained the four lower bridges were to be employed in maintaining a pavement six yards wide in the middle of the highway between the Market Cross, which stood where Castle Street joined the High Street, and Church Lane. The Wardens thereafter abided by the spirit, if not the letter, of that Decree.

When the Elizabethan Indenture was drawn up, roads in towns were rarely surfaced, and outside of towns were rarely defined. The Medway valley flooded after rain, and in winter, the clay roads of the Weald became impassable morasses.

Many landowners left bequests for the repair of the roads they had struggled over during their lives. John Judde by his will of 1492, left money to the 'mending of foul ways most needful in Tonbridge, Speldhurst and Penshurst'. Richard Mylls by his will of 1531 gave lands near to Lodge Oak to repair the road between Vauxhall and Tonbridge Town; his Charity, known as the Waylands, is now amalgamated with the Town Wardens.

The relief that such Charities gave to parishioners who were responsible for perilous stretches of highway was substantial, and for centuries to concentrate the benefits of the Lands on the place where they lived, the Town Wardens ignored the rest of the vast Parish and jealously confined their activities to the small area they knew as 'Tonbridge Town' and the waterlogged highway which ran from the Great Bridge to the Angel and the former Priory.

The Wardens

Many of the Wardens came from families that had been in the town for generations. The family names which appear as Wardens, tenants, creditors and debtors also appear in the Vestry, and Court Leet records as Churchwardens, Surveyors of Highways, and other parish officers. Churchwardens were elected annually, and Town Wardens for a three year term. Between 1714 and 1830 the same family name appears 83 times in the annual list of Churchwardens and 72 times in the list of Town Wardens.

The Wardens were chosen from folk of the middling sort: members of families who owned large estates such as Childrens, Wellers and Woodgates; farmers and millers; professional men such as Scoones; officials and minor gentry; and large and small tradesmen and craftsmen. The signatures of witnesses at the passing of the accounts, and the names in the accounts, remind us that the population of the 'Town' was small, and that all the townsfolk were well known to each other and connected by ties of family, marriage, friendship, employment or interest. It is little wonder that in such a close-knit community, in the club-like atmosphere of the discussions at the Angel, the Bull, the Castle or the Crown, where it was not unknown for the Landlord to be a Warden, there was little disagreement about what was good for the town.

The Lands

The total area of the lands as given in the earliest lettings varies around 31½ acres against the 30 acres of the Decree. Later surveys show the total area was 39 acres, 3 roods, 12 perches (16.12 hectares). Almost exactly two thirds of the area was arable; the remainder was meadow where ploughing was always prohibited on pain of a penal increase in rent.

The conditions of letting were simple: the tenant had to enter into a bond, the timber was reserved to the Wardens – though the tenant was allowed hedgebote (sufficient loppings to repair the boundary fences), and the tenant was not to 'streepe nor waste the land'. Through the years the conditions were added to and specified in more prolix detail, until late in the eighteenth century a lease expanded to occupy two full 'skins' of parchment with a consequential increase in lawyers' fees.

The only parcel north of the Medway is Brightfriars Meadow. The River divides to surround the Racecourse and the meadow lies

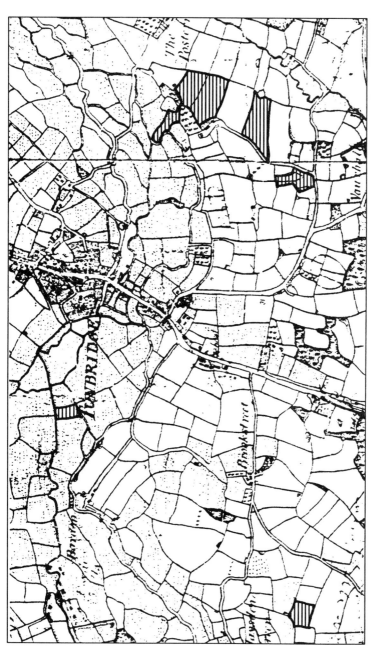

Tonbridge and the surrounding area at the end of the eighteenth century, showing the location of the Town Lands, shaded thus:

(Source: based on 3" O. S. draft map of 1799, by permission of the British Library: OSD 100 pt2 (Ser 352))

between the left bank of the northern branch and the footpath from The Slade to Hayesden. Iron markers 'T W' define the straightening of a former irregular boundary, and until it was cultivated in World War II it had always been untouched meadow.

The most westerly parcel, also meadow, is on the north side of Upper Hayesden Lane. Local readers will know it as Yeomans, the Judd School rugby field east of the A21 Tonbridge Bypass.

Three parcels in the angle on the north side of Tudeley Lane and the west side of Lodge Oak Lane were usually let together. One was meadow, and part of the northern boundary is the footpath which crosses the east end of Kings Road. The sale of oak trees from this group brought a welcome addition to the Wardens' funds.

The largest single parcel called 'The Great' was north of the Cardinal's Error on the east side of Lodge Oak Lane; it ran down to Priory Mill. Council houses were built on part, and the shallow pits from which marl was taken can still be seen on the allotments east of the houses.

In 1700 the northern branch of the Medway curved south across the present waterworks site to rejoin the southern branch northeast of where Buley's weir was built in 1850. The re-united streams flowed under the Lower Bridge and onwards parallel to the present Vale Road. Part of the Town Lands meadow now occupied by the Sewage Treatment Plant and commercial premises bordered the river. The arable land rose south east from the meadow and was crossed by the track which ran from the Great Bridge to Postern Forge.

With the exception of Brightfriars Meadow, the Town Lands were near to roads which may have been used by generous donors whose identities are still mysteries. The last of the Lands was sold in 1950.

The Town

Tonbridge town has grown up on a spur of hard clay jutting into the flood plain which the Medway is cutting as it meanders to the sea. From earliest times travellers have rested on this south facing slope as they waited for this, the shortest route across the valley, to dry out.

Eighteenth-century travellers noted two features in Tonbridge. The first was outside the School where a causeway was raised above the rough rutted carriageway and separated from it by posts and rails. This comparatively safe dry smooth footpath was noteworthy in an age when pedestrians usually shared the roads with sheep, pigs, and cattle, and with horsemen, carts, carriages and wagons which churned up and deeply rutted the surface. Below the school, on the east side of the road, a house called 'Chauntlers' faced the Church across the water-filled town ditch. To the west the ditch was dry, and on its north side a stile closed the end of a footpath to the Potkiln Farm and Hilden Bridge.

The bridge over the town ditch was about 13 feet wide, and the first house on the east – the timber framed house now known as the Ivy House – was reputed to be the guard house of the bridge; it was formerly known as the Elephant and Castle. Between the guard house and the Red Lyon at the corner of Church Lane was the Bull Inn. This narrow stretch of road was described as 'Bull Street' when the Wardens worked here, and when the Bull moved down to the south of the Great Bridge the name 'Bull Street' moved with it. On the west side of the road were orchards, barns, and houses (between two of them was a walled and roofed well, with two rolls and two buckets – one for each house). One of the parties to the Indenture had lived here and had a small paved area outside his door.

At Church Lane the road divided. The right hand branch (Bank Street) led to the castle barbican and the town pound, and thence around the outer bailey to the end of the town ditch at the Hawden stream. The waters of the Hawden Stream and Hilden Brook were not allowed to flow into the old Medway but by weirs and sluices fed the castle moat and the Lord's Mill. (The new canal between the castle and Buley's weir was not cut until 1829.) The left hand branch of the road (the High Street) was lined with houses, hostelries and shops with stables, workshops or brewhouses in their yards; over the shops were living rooms for family and servants. Towards the half timbered Rose and Crown the street grew wide enough for the pens and stalls for the markets and fairs to be put up.

88

In this stretch of road was the second notable feature of the town; it was the six yard wide paved strip in the otherwise unpaved road between Church Lane and the Market Cross, and it was well known to be the responsibility of the Town Wardens.

But for these two lengths of paving and a few small patches outside house doors, the roads were not paved as we understand the term. ('Paving' in the early days of the Charity meant a surface which had been levelled and strengthened by being strewn with stones which were then stamped or rammed down into the soft earth.)

The triangle bounded by the High Street, Bank Street and Castle Street had once been 'common mead' – a 'village green' complete with pond (Luck's Pool). By Georgian times permanent buildings had replaced the former booths and stalls, but reminders of common use were the Cage or Lock-up at the top of Castle Street and the public draw well at the bottom.

The centre of the town was where Castle Street met the High Street, and was marked by the Market Cross. This had been rebuilt in 1671 with four low brick walls and stout timber corner posts supporting a pitched tiled roof of four gables. At the north end, on a six feet high brick base, was a three-storied clock tower of white painted shiplap boarding crowned by a beehive bell turret and weathercock.

From the Market Cross, East Street ran past the bottom of Church Street, through the hill on which the Church had been built, to a sandstone bridge across the town ditch – here filled with willow beds. Leaning high over the bridge was a large timber framed house, reputed to be the guardhouse of the East Street bridge and now called the Portreeve's House. It had formerly been known as the Old Ivy House.

The town ditch completed its enclosing protective circuit through the hill to the mill stream. East Street beyond the bridge was known as Mill Lane or Swan Lane, and continued along the edge of the Medway flood plain to Hadlow and Maidstone.

The Market Cross was not only part of the market; it was also the site of public punishments. Here were the stocks and whipping post (paid for by the Wardens in Queen Anne's days), here Wat Tyler's brother was reputed to have been hung, and here martyrs and poisoners had been burned.

From the Cross to the Great Bridge a steep and deep channel ran down past the shops and the Chequers where the Manor Court was sometimes held. The channel was offensive to eye and nose, for only after heavy rain was it washed clear of the butchers' refuse, dung, market rubbish and filth which clogged it.

An easy slope ran into the water on the upstream side of the long bridge which spanned not the main river, but the waters of the moat and mill stream. South of the bridge the land was several feet lower than today, and the water level for the moat and mill was kept up by an artificial bank, which the miller was obliged to keep in good repair. At the foot of the slope by the bridge the Wardens maintained a platform of stone and timber for people to dip for water and do their washing. Carts were driven into the water here to allow the cattle to drink and to tighten the joints of the cart wheels. Commanding the Great Bridge was the remains of the four storey high Watergate Tower of the castle.

To our Georgian ancestors 'Town' was the 35 acres bounded by the town ditch and the mill stream. Within 'Town' most buildings, with the exception of such symbols of power as the castle and the church, with its cement-rendered tower, were of timber and wattle and daub, or were clad in painted shiplap. Some roofs were tiled and the church was shingle covered, but the poorer houses were small and thatched. The intimate scale is difficult to imagine. Roads were just wide enough to take a horse or oxen-drawn cart. Castle Street and Church Lane are typical roads of a period when slow moving carters had time to give way to each other.

By means of weirs and sluices landowners took water to their premises by three artificial channels braided together between the mill stream and the main river. Tanners washed their skins in the streams; hemp and flax were retted (left to soak) in them to separate the fibres, and brewers and blacksmiths needed water. In the country-side below the town waterways were impeded by fish weirs, eel traps, mills, fallen trees and other obstructions. In these circumstances a little rainfall was enough to flood the valley and the town and its roads for days.

The first charge on the Wardens' profits was the repair of the bridges over the three artificial lower streams and the main river. Locally the bridges were known by the names of the people who lived nearby, and as generation gave way to generation the names of the bridges changed. Reports on the bridges made by 'foreigners' to the town cause confusion: the Great Bridge may or may not be included, and the numbering may be from north to south or vice versa.

South of the Great Bridge the narrow road was like a switchback. The hump-backed bridges reared over the streams in quick succession. All had originally been stone arches and eleven feet wide, but by 1777 each had been widened in stages to about seventeen feet. Thirty yards or so south of the foot of the Great Bridge was the crown of the 'Loggerheads' bridge; 50 yards beyond that was the crown of 'Sutton's' bridge; after another 70 yards 'Osbourne's' lifted the road steeply over the 'back stream of the Medway', and finally, 55 yards farther on, up an equally inconveniently steep slope, was the crown of the fifth or Lower Bridge of two arches spanning the main river Medway. Steps on the upstream side of that bridge led to the waterside and a platform or stage   the second 'dipping place' or 'washing place' maintained by the Wardens.

The ground between the bridges regularly flooded and would have been impassable in winter but for 'the clappers'. These were wooden walkways, some with handrails, and were used by pedestrians and horsemen and maintained by the Wardens.

The Angel, an old hostelry, marked the end of the High Street. Here was a large fishpond, part of the Priory. The road divided around it. The road to Rye swung east past the main Priory buildings (now the railway car park), and climbed southeast on the line of Commercial Street across the later lavender fields and over Primrose Hill; thence it dipped into the valley to cross the Somerhill Stream east of Vauxhall, and rose again on its way over Castle Hill, past the remains of the Iron Age fort, to Rye and the Continent.

The other branch swung west of the fish pond, and after a short distance split into two roads and a footpath. One road ran west along the bank on the edge of the flood plain to the sandstone bluff at Barden; the footpath headed to Brook Street Farm and the other road wandered up the present Waterloo Road to face the steep climb up Quarry Hill to the old village of Bidborough and on through the hamlet of Southborough to the fashionable Wells at the far end of the parish.

All highway bridges were the responsibility of the County unless it could be shown that another body should bear the burden. Highways were the responsibility of the inhabitants of the parish. The parishioners at a meeting of 'The Vestry' elected many parish officers, including Surveyors of Highways for the four 'Boroughs' into which the parish was divided. Their duties were to ensure the inhabitants did their duty. The Surveyors for the 'Borough of Town' at one time directed the Town Wardens. A Court Leet (a court of the Lord of the Manor) had jurisdiction over markets and fairs and dealt with highway damage, obstructions, nuisances and encroachments; the Court sometimes elected the Wardens. Turnpike Trustees collected tolls for the maintenance of some main roads outside the towns. The miles of parish roads beyond the Angel might not have existed so far as the Wardens were concerned. The Angel was the limit of their interest.

The Income

The rents from the lands provided the Wardens with most of their money. A small proportion of timber from the Lodge Oak lands was used to repair the clappers, dipping places and bridges, but at intervals varying between ten and thirty years, a handsome periodic boost to the funds came from selling timber, the tan (bark used in tanning) and the toppings. Infrequently small sums came in from selling road stone – stockpiled at an unknown 'Great Yard', and occasionally the Surveyor of Highways gave money for work.

The Rents

The rents quoted here are those bid at auction, but they are not always the amounts received. The Wardens were always tender to sick tenants and widows, and some deductions from rents were made for a variety of reasons: Church Rate, 'Poor Cease' (a local tax or rate normally spelt 'Cess' and abbreviated from the word 'As-sess-ment'), Tythes, Bridge Money (a contribution for the repair of County bridges), Gaol Rate (for building the prison at Maidstone), 'St Andrew's Aide' (which occurs rarely and was probably a traditional fee due to the Lord of the Manor. It appears in a document in 1314) and 'Land Tax and wine' – the wine probably being drunk when the rent was received.

In the early years of the Charity the leases were for three years; later the term of years and the conditions varied.

The following list of yearly rents reflects the effect of national events on the economy through Georgian times:

	£	s	d	
1575	13	0	0	
1689	20	0	0	
1711-1720	20	0	0	
1720-1735	22	0	0	
1735-1750	25	0	0	One tenant had all the lands.
1750-1765	31	0	0	
1765-1781	37	17	0	To be paid at the Rose and Crown.
1781-1796	43	15	0	
1796-1811	62	0	0	
1811-1823	159	10	0	1811-35: Because of bankrupt-
	129	10	0	cies, deaths, assignments and
	126	0	0	refusals to pay, the Wardens did
	112	15	0	not receive all these rents. See
1823-1835	69	0	0	following notes.

At Michaelmas 1765 when Thomas Swayne, the Steward of the Court, auctioned the lands at the Manor Court they fetched £37 17s a year which was an increase of 22 per cent over the former rent.

Swayne's charge to the Wardens for preparing the leases and for some other items was £6 4s. At Michaelmas 1780 the increase of about 15 per cent in the total rent to £43 15s was in line with the trend which had been evident for several years.

From the execution of Louis XVI in January 1793 until Nelson's victory off Cape St Vincent in 1797 there was gloom and depression in the country. Harvests were bad, the Bank of England – unable to pay in specie – issued Bank Notes, the Navy in the Medway mutinied, the country remained threatened with invasion, and the Funds fell to unheard of levels. Despite this depression, when the lands were auctioned in January 1796, the total bids came to £62 a year – 42 per cent more than the sitting tenants were paying. Inflation continued to rise during the French Wars, and was reflected in a spirit of almost reckless optimism fifteen years later in 1811 when the lands were next auctioned. They then fetched £159 10s a year – an increase of 157 per cent over the 1796 rents.

Between the false peace of Amiens in 1802 and the death of George III in 1822, despite national triumphs, the personal and financial disasters to respected and substantial townsmen of standing in this period made it one of misery, despair and uncertainty in Tonbridge. In 1812 the Tonbridge Bank failed and in May 1815 the other bank, The Tonbridge New Bank, of Mercer and Barlow closed its doors. The exultation of the victory of Waterloo evaporated, and was followed by internal stress and discontent as trade languished due to the exhaustion of the countries of Europe and their inability to buy our goods.

The Wardens' income fell. There was effectively no summer in 1816; the harvest was bad and there were severe floods. In October, on the death of George Butler, a tenant whose rent had been paid by assigns, the Lodge Oak Lands were re-auctioned. They were re-let to John Keat for four years for £25 and he failed too, and paid no more than ten shillings in the pound. In December, with riots in the country, the lands of Major Woodgate were put up for auction, and although William Bailey, the new owner of the castle, took over Brightfriars at the old rent of £15, The Great fetched only £14 against the Major's £44. Isaac Uridge was also in trouble with his rents. By re-lets the notional £159 10s had fallen to a notional £112 10s a year but how much of this was received is hidden from us.

On 5 February 1823, after 200 advertising bills had been printed and distributed, the lands were put up for auction for 12 years. A measure of the change since 1811 is that after brisk bidding the new rents brought in only £69 a year. Scoones charges for the bills, the auction and half the cost of preparing the leases was £27 15s 8d – he settled for £27.

Other income
The accounts for 1717-20 show two of the minor items of income:

> Recd of Mr Twort for Tann from the Towne Lands   00:11:00
> recd by rubbidge Stones left in paving the bridges   00:07:00

The second is simply from the sale of small quantities of stones, but the first illuminates commercial life in the town. As we have seen, use was made of the timber from the Town Lands, and the Wardens also did well out of the smaller pollard wood, cutting and selling it by the cord, and making up for sale 232 faggots (bundles) with 'wifths'. 'Mr Twort' was a tanner, and the trees in this case were almost certainly oak. When the tree was felled, the bark was flawed (that is, flayed or stripped off) and bundled into six foot strips ('fathoms') – this was 'the Tann' and Mr Twort used it in his tanning vats. When leather was in great demand for accoutrements for soldiers the price of the tann could be as much as a third of the price of the whole tree.

Tanning was, and is, an offensive trade, and tanners need water; they were often banished to the lee side of towns. There are references to tanners in Tonbridge from 1555, and always where they could use the water downstream of the washing and dipping places. Mr Twort occupied the four acres downstream of the mill, bounded by the stream, Garden Road, the road to Hadlow, and Mill Lane. Until the 1960s a barn constructed in 1802 stood at the bottom of the site. The first floor where the skins hung had ingenious but

simple contrivances for opening the whole of the walls to the venti-
lating winds, and was a reminder of what the site had been used for
by Mr Twort and his successors.

Trees were sometimes cut into slabs where they fell, and accounts
show items for digging and refilling the pit for the sawing. In this case
the felling and flawing of the timber from which the tann came took
Edward Hilman and William Curd two and a half days at one shilling
and tenpence a day each; not the craftsman rate, but more than an
unskilled labourer earned. In 1699 three trees were sold for £5; in
1709 an exceptional tree brought in £2 7s 6d. In April 1749, 60
were sold for £75, equal to a doubling of the income for that three
year term of office (although one failed to get to the purchaser and he
had his £1 5s back); in 1780 timber brought in £47 5s. and in 1811
an unknown number of trees brought in £94.

Expenditure

Introduction

The Wardens spent most of their income on pavings. In the early
eighteenth century that involved seeking, buying and moving stones;
breaking, spreading and ramming them, and paying for the tools to
be repaired. When necessary they repaired the structure and copings
of the four narrow bridges, and at two of the bridges they kept the
dipping places safe. They repaired the clappers, and when these were
swept away by ice or floods they rescued them; and to protect
pedestrians they put up and painted posts and rails. They were always
generous with liquid refreshment when they were chosen, when
work was done, when the rents were received or when they sold
trees. When the accounts were passed any odd amounts of cash in
hand were frequently soaked up in the same way.

The pattern of approval to most sets of accounts runs on the
following lines (for 1735-38): 'these accounts were seen and allow'd,
and the accountants haveing expended foar shillings and foar pence
the accounts are even – wittness our Hands ...'.

Not all the income was spent on productive work. In the early days the Wardens overspent almost casually, and were paid by the next Wardens when money came to hand. On the rare occasion when payment was delayed for several years a Warden was repaid with interest. If rents came in slowly, tradesmen might be paid in instalments or have to wait as long as four years. When the first successful local Bank began to be used these delays ceased and creditors were paid by the Bank. By the time of George IV the Bank held all the Wardens' money and a new item of expenditure was 'Interest'.

As the end of the century approached the Land Tax on the Town Lands was redeemed at a total cost, including legal fees, of £55 13s 2d and a more formal mode appears with money being spent on receipt stamps, letters, making up the accounts, elaborate leases and other legal fees.

The cash available to each set of Wardens varied considerably depending on how much was in hand and any exceptional income. Expenditure depended on what needed doing, the weather, and the vigour of the Wardens.

The accounts were not drawn up with a view to being analysed. Some accounts separate 'paving' from 'paving the bridges'; others do not separate work to the bridges from the dipping places and steps which were part of the same structure. Nevertheless a rough idea of how much was spent on different types of works can be gleaned from the papers. There is no doubt the bridges had first priority, and about a tenth of the available money was spent on them, but how much was structural and how much paving over them is doubtful. The repair of the clappers was a constant task but took little money, and until 1792, when another item began to appear, the balance of the money spent on works went on paving. Over the Georgian period that proportion may have varied from 40 to 97 per cent in each term, with an approximate average over the period of two thirds. A typical example of a sheet of accounts is given in Appendix 3.

Pavings

In 1711 the town roads were unbelievably bad. Deep pot-holes and water-filled ruts traced the paths of waggons through a mixture of mud, stones and rubbish which made the passage through the streets hazardous and uncomfortable. As late as 1750 maintenance was no more than putting stones into the ruts, pot-holes, and puddles. By then some of the 'paved' footways made by ramming the stones into the soil had been edged with shallow depressions or gutters of stone, but as we have seen, such high quality 'pavements' were so rare as to be worthy of note.

There were complaints at the Court Leet that dung, butchers' offal, and other refuse was flung onto the roads and chamber pots were emptied from windows. There were no drains, the roofs of houses had no gutters and water fell on passers by. In such conditions roads were easily damaged by heavy loads and there was legislation about the width and spacing of the waggon wheels – the wide wheels were the means by which the stones were crushed into the mud and refuse covering the road. The nearest source of stone was the river, but such stone was soft, and was quickly crushed to mud. In wet weather it washed away and in dry weather it blew away as dust.

The early accounts do not show where stones came from, and as the price may or may not include carriage, true costs are uncertain. The names of vendors of small quantities of stone suggest that local farmers who collected or dug stones from their land sold them to the Wardens. In the 1711-14 term, stone was bought at 6s a load (plus an item for bread and beer money making another 4d a load); loads of gravel cost between 1s 2d and 2s 6d a load and the terms 'Tons' and 'Loads' were often interchangeable. At these prices the stone was of a quality worth bringing from a distance, that is, it was harder than the gravel won from the river or from a nearby farm.

The bridges were always the first places where higher quality stones and better methods of paving were used. A 1719 entry is the first about an important improvement: 'grett stones' were bought at 7s a load. The new stone was probably rag, and it was laid over the bridges to give an irregular but tight surface. The Wardens paid half the cost – the rest may have been paid by the Waylands Charity, the Highway Surveyor, or by Roger Strange who repaved 194 yards of the Great Bridge for the County between 1721 and 1723.

A single entry in 1735-8 refers to stone from 'Roffway' (in Plaxtol – about four and a half miles north of Tonbridge). It was therefore ragstone – a good quality stone; at 3s 6d a load the carriage must have been paid for separately. When laid, the surface would not have been smooth and flat, but what today would be regarded as cobblestones.

By April 1749 one effect of the canalisation of the Medway up to the Great Bridge becomes apparent in the documents. Gravel, ragstone and sand were coming up the river in larger quantities and of higher quality and lower price than had ever been available by horse and cart. For the same money the Wardens could then do more work and with more durable stone.

A docket records the first of many payments to the Medway Navigation Company. It is undated and states:

To Thomas Scoones for Stones and Gravel of the Compy River Midway 2 bills	£22: 3: 6

The earliest surviving docket supporting any payment is also in these accounts. Like so many others it is a small piece of paper 6½ inches by 3½ inches. It states:

Sept 13 1745	Mr. Wiffen three Load of Gravel	0:07: 06
Octr 29	Two load of gravel	0:05: 00
		0:12: 06

Rcd of Mr. Wiffen the full of this Bill
Georg Walter

At the same time George Barnaby was paid 12s 6d for 'fetching Stones and gravel from ye Warf'.

The produce of the Tonbridge area was now easily taken down river, and not only road stone, but coal, chalk and other materials were brought upstream in quantities undreamed of before. The new goods arriving at the Wharf, and the local produce going away, boosted all trade and created an optimistic air in the town. The improvement in roads was country-wide, and travel by horseback and carriage by packhorse began to give way to wheeled vehicles. The increase in traffic was destructive to the town roads and the bridges, and demanded more maintenance work. Fortunately, as their accounts for the next five years show, the Wardens were benefiting from the changes, and surviving dockets give details of the source of the stones, from whom they were bought, where they were used, and the dimensions of the paving and gutters laid.

A comparison of some costs in the accounts of the Wardens John Lines and James Norris (1753-58) with earlier ones is illuminating:

1754		£: s: d
Octo 31	Pd Mr. Thos Scoones junr for ye Medway Company for 70 Tons of Stones & 102 Tun of Gravil as per Bill	20:17: 0
1755		
May 31	Pd Thos Eliott for fetching Two Load of Stones from Prats Quarry	0:10: 0
July 5	Pd George Pratt for Two load of San Ston to Mend ye Lower Bridge	0: 6: 0
June 30	Pd Mr Scoones for 35 Ton of Stones & 43 Ton & ½ of Gravil	10: 1: 0
Decr 31	Pd Mr Scoones for 64 Ton of Stones & 31 Ton of Gravil	15:19: 0

The previous price for stone had been 6s or 7s a ton. Now, not only was good gravel 1s, and the stone 4s 6d a ton, but they were available within a short distance of where they were to be used. Instead of horses taking all day to trundle and struggle through the clay lanes to Plaxtol or Ightham for a cart load, 20 or more tons at a time were arriving at the Wharf. The new stones came from Maidstone where they were quarried; they were the same special 'grett' stone – the rag stone – formerly bought from Roughway or Plaxtol. The sandstone bought from George Pratt, at 8s a ton delivered to the site, was for a bridge – not suitable for road stone and not to be compared with the first Medway Company roadstone. Paving was usually charged at 3d a (square) yard. If charged at 4d a yard it is likely the ground was being levelled before the stone was spread, thus indicating paved areas were being extended. Stone continued to be broken and spread on the roads, but between 1756 and 1759 the whole length was paved between the Lower Bridge and the Turnpike (Gate) – that is

_1759_ Brought Foreward   21 . 18 . 11

May 30 Paid Mr David Sherlock for
Carpentors Work &c. as ∯ Bill — 0 . 16 . 8
31 Paid Thos Mercer for Paving of
Dryland Crossway as ∯ Bill — 0 . 4 . 2
31 Paid Mr Thos Seoons on account
of the Company of the River Medway
for Stones and Gravell as ∯ Recceit 10 . 0 . 0
Sep^tr 10 Paid Thos Penson for Mending at
_1759_ the Logerhead Bridge — 0 . 0 . 6
Feb^ry 2 Paid Mr Wm Johnson as ∯ Bill — 0 . 2 . 5
March 24 Paid Mr Thos Seoons for account
of the Company of the River Medway 20 . 0 . 0
August 28 Paid Thos Mercer — as ∯ Bill — 0 . 12 . 0
Octr 31 Paid Thos Mercer — as ∯ Bill 2 . 12 . 10
Novr 14 Paid John Grenaway for Spreading
Stones — 0 . 1 . 2
28 Paid Mr David Sherlock for Work
Done — as ∯ Bill 0 . 13 . 2
28 Paid Mr Wm Johnson Blacksmith
— as ∯ Bill — 0 . 6 . 1
28 Paid Jacob Mercer for Mending
Part of the Logerhead Bridge — 0 . 1 . 6
57 . 9 . 3

A typical extract from the Wardens' account book.
At this time, in the early years of the Seven Years War, Admiral Byng
had been shot and Clive and Wolfe were being successful in India and
North America. In Tonbridge this year a new sundial was bought for
the Parish Church.

to the Angel. The width varied between fifteen feet and eighteen feet which correlates well with the width given for the Lower Bridge and shows the carriageway was paved too. As the rate was 4d a yard new paving is indicated.

At the beginning of the new reign in 1760 the Wardens ventured beyond their traditional limit of Church Lane by 'laying stones in ye Road near the Red Lyon' (that is the north corner of the lane). For the first twenty years of the reign their work was routine. Thomas Mercer continued paving at the old rate of 3d a square yard; frequently in strips. He paved a strip about 12 feet wide from the Market Cross to the Great Bridge; a strip in Swan Lane and Mr Scoones's Bridge (perhaps over the Fosse in East Street); a strip under three yards wide from Church Lane to the Market Cross, and a strip about six feet six inches wide from the Lower Bridge to the Turnpike Gate at the Angel. In three years towards the end of the 1760s almost three thousand square yards of paving were laid (all but about five hundred yards being paid for by the Wardens). It cost them £92 and exhausted their funds.

Another step forward was recorded in May 1774. For the first time 'heded' stone was bought – stones that had at least one end squared so they might be laid to give an even surface. They came up the river from Samuel Weeks' ragstone quarries near Maidstone at '3s 9d ye Tun', and were the first improvement noted over the old rough cobbles. Thomas Mercer was paid for mending and 'sloping the trades between the bridges and near the lower bridge'. The Oxford English Dictionary gives 'trades' as a Kentishism for a track or wheel tread, and he may have been setting the 'heded' stones as gutters.

In 1775 the River Company dealt in stones which had not come up the river – hard stones (chert) from Plaxtol for example at 8s a load, and carriage of stone charged for by the day. The Company charged 3d a load for weighing stones but as no weights are given, the number of tons in a load is not known.

Between 1775 and 1780 when the Wardens again paved from the Lower Bridge to the Angel the width had increased to eighteen feet. That they paid for breaking the stones on the site is indicated by the entry:

Pd Uridge for damage to a window by breaking Stones   1s 10d

The Medway Company was thriving in 1780; horse traffic crowded the streets and the Wharf, and the day to day pattern of the Wardens' work continued as before until George Jeffery and Samuel Ollive became Wardens at Michaelmas 1789. This was the year in which the storming of the Bastille was greeted with delight in England. The winter was severe, the Thames froze over and there was great distress in the country. The Wardens received no money from their predecessors until June. It is likely the roads were broken up by the frost as in October 1790 the Wardens began to pay for breaking stones and for paving from Bordyke to the Angel. The work continued until the end of June 1792 and payment was made week by week.

In 1798 Mr William Woodgate, the Lord of the Manor, made a change which altered the appearance and the character of the town. He demolished the much loved Market Cross and replaced it by a symbol of the Georgian age, a brick Town Hall, which like the new castle house, was not universally admired. The ground floor of the new building was open, and the south end of the first floor room was slightly bowed. The account book says nothing of alterations to the paving around the Town Hall but includes the following items:

Horse & expenses to buy stones (3 times)		1. 7. 6.
Ditto to Farley after stones		12. 0.
John Hutson (sent in the Tonbridge barge by Revd Mark Noble) 25½ Tons of Headed Stones at 7s the Ton		8.18. 6.
Medway Coy (2 bills) paving and stones		24.10.10.
James Pope for paving (4 bills)		91.14. 0½
Measuring the paving		15. 0.
R. Evenden (4 bills) including 11 loads of stones @ 24s a load		29. 9. 6.
Beer for workmen (3 bills)		2.10.
G. Noakes. Liquor at different times		12. 8.
Gibeon Noakes		7. 6½
Thos Fox. 8 pots of beer	3. 4	
Ditto 4 Lownes to the Stone Waggon	6. 0	9. 4.

Once again the paving was of a higher standard than before. The ragstones bought from the Revd Mark Noble of Farleigh and brought to the Wharf in the Tonbridge barge by Mr Hutson, were trimmed paving blocks which could be laid with smaller joints. The cost of laying them was 9d a square yard and with bills from other paviors, the conclusion is that a length of well over 400 yards of the High Street was repaved at the time the new Town Hall was built. At the end of their term the Wardens had only £5 9s 0½d left to pass on to their successors.

The opening of the reign of George IV in 1820 brought more improvements for pedestrians. A sketch on the back of a bill shows gutters of squared ragstone blocks with tight joints supporting the edges of the carriageway, and squared ragstone curbs supporting the footways and backing the gutters. A footway had been made when the Lower Bridge was rebuilt in 1814, and in 1818 the stone parapets of the Great Bridge had been replaced by iron railings to widen the footway, but generally footways and carriageways had been separated only by the hollow gutters.

Despite their income being erratic, the Wardens bought and laid York stone paving over the three lower bridges. York stone is flat squared slabs of hard sandstone, which can be laid evenly with tight joints and to gentle falls to carry away water. The new work was superior to anything seen before, but it was expensive. One mason earned 5s 4d a day, and his labourer 3s 6d. Mr Sutton who supplied the stone and men, wrote many letters dealing with the price and the advantages of dressing the stones before sending them to Tonbridge by either waggon or barge.

As the Wardens had no funds to pay for these superior pavings Mr Sutton had difficulties. He was paid bit by bit, the last instalment in August 1822 after he had come to Tonbridge market to meet the Wardens. He was allowed to attend the Court Leet and witness the accounts in 1822. The first 'chack' (cheque) found in the accounts, on Beechings Bank, is made out to him. It is a simple document – a piece of plain writing paper 7½ by 2½ inches, on which John Luckhurst has scribbled:

Tonbridge   Jan 16 1820
To   Messrs Beeching & Son
          Tonbridge Bank
Gnm. please pay Mr. Sutton
or Bearer Fortynine pounds
13 shillings & 9d for
Your most obed. Svt.
£49.13.9   John Luckhurst

Road maintenance was no longer the simple act of throwing stones
into pot holes and ruts. With materials of different types, qualities,
and methods of laying being used, all at different prices, the measuring and appraisal of the quantities and qualities became too specialised for the layman, and John King and his partner, Brown, were
often called in to supervise the work, measure it, and settle the
account. They charged 2½ per cent of the cost.

As for paying for the work, that too became less simple than
handing over a guinea or so when the rents came in. As noted,
despite having no money to pay Mr Sutton, the Wardens went ahead
with the expensive paving, and that first 'chack' which did not
appear in the accounts for another twelve months, and items for
'Interest paid', signal a more sophisticated approach to their financial
affairs.

Messrs Beeching's Bank was in the High Street on the south
corner of Church Lane. He and his Bank had been of great help to
the tradesmen and the Wardens, and he benefited from the new
standards. The area by his Bank had been paved with York stone and
in 1823, 339 feet 7 inches was relaid at a cost of £2 2s 5d (1½d a foot
– an unusual unit). It was measured by King and Brown.

Continuing the good work, in 1824 the Town Surveyor macadamised the carriageway over three of the lower bridges and the
Wardens found the money for the work. McAdam's method was to
break stones to such a size that they could go into one's mouth. They
were then laid over the carriageway in a smooth heavily cambered
profile about four inches thick to allow the rain water to drain away
quickly; a slurry of soil, sand, and water was brushed into the surface
to hold the stones together, but the consolidation was still done by

the broad wheels of the waggons. When finished, the surface of the road over the lower bridges, supported by the gutters and kerbs, was better than any other section of road in the town.

A macadamised surface was so much smoother than the old roads that lighter and therefore swifter carriages could be used. The surface had to be kept sound and in good shape, as in dry weather it became dusty and broke up, and in wet or frosty weather any hollows filled with water or ice, and the surface broke away and the road was lost. After the Georgian period the Wardens had to buy a water cart and hire a roller to maintain the surface.

This was not the end of improvements being made – for instance in November 1825 when John Luckhurst was chosen for his third term with Mr Robert Mercer as his fellow Warden they purchased eight feet of 'Grannett' curb at one shilling and elevenpence a foot. It had been found to weigh 5 cwt by Mr Winchester, the carrier. Later they bought some circular granite curb and paid for it to be worked and jointed. The rate for the masons was 5s 2d and they were paid eightpence for 'tules'. Granite, which in this case came to Maidstone by boat from Cornwall, and then by barge to the town wharf, is much harder than any of the local stones. To work it needs better tools, more frequently sharpened; hence the additional charge. The granite withstands the wear of the ironshod wheels of waggons, and is especially valuable at corners and at bridges. It is well worth the extra cost its weight and the difficulty of working it entails. Some can be seen at the bridge at the bottom of Mill Lane.

In the last years of the reign 'Fur stones' and clinker were bought from Sevenoaks. 'Fire stone' may have been chert, referred to as 'Sevenoaks stone' in tenders for the purchase of road stone. When struck it produces a fire or spark similar to flint. The details of the clinker are not known.

The last entry dealing with pavings in John Luckhurst's accounts is for 19 October 1826, by which time when he journeyed to Ightham to buy stones for the Town he had to hire a chaise from his old partner, the former Warden James Arrow.

Expenditure on Bridges, Dipping Places and Clappers

Bridges. Money was spent on these important structures every year, but there is no way of apportioning the amounts accurately. Payments for the use of scaffolding and centres (semi-circular timber framed temporary supports), confirm that the stone arches were repaired many times. Sandstone for the work was bought from the castle and elsewhere, and lime and lead were bought when the copings were repaired. Stones were also brought in to reduce the steep slopes to the hump-backs which were always a nuisance.

The arch of the bridge over the 'back stream of the river', that is the one next to the Lower Bridge, had been repaired in 1809, and was in good condition when, at Michaelmas 1813, John King began his third term as Warden, this term with William Town as his partner. They had an unhappy time. Their accounts, which were never approved, include a bill from Mr John King himself for 'Temporary Bridge & other Expenses Relating to the same £235.8.7½'.

The Wardens' documents and John King's own notes tell the story behind this heavy bill. January 1814 was a month of bitter cold. On Saturday 29th the river and the side streams were frozen and the ice was thick. When a sudden thaw set in, the ice broke up and large floes swept down the river and the back stream. They jammed in the arches of both the lower bridges, punched two holes in the arch of the back stream bridge which temporarily relieved the pressure, and at about nine in the morning swept away the Lower Bridge.

John King spent the rest of the day at the site with his fellow Warden William Town, the Surveyor of Highways, the Constable, and other leading townsmen. On Sunday 30th as the waters were falling, King and Town surveyed the damaged remains and conferred over three bottles of warm wine provided by Mr Parker at a cost of a guinea.

The gap was fenced off and lit to make it temporarily safe, and in the following week King bought ropes, heavy timber, scaffold boards and heavy spikes, and employed carpenters bricklayers and labourers to clear the debris and put a temporary footbridge across the gap. His notes say the mail and stage coaches were diverted, some through the

Postern and some through Penshurst and Leigh, and that the stock market was held on both sides of the river.

In the meantime on Friday, 4 February, King attended the Magistrates (which cost five shillings) and on Saturday reached agreement with Mr Charles Willard, the owner of the land on the east side of the gap, to build a temporary bridge and road over his land. King had reason to be pleased with the arrangements he had made, but on the Sunday, when he spent £2 10s on sending a messenger to London on an unspecified errand, Mr Willard resiled from the agreement, and eventually the temporary bridge and road necessary to enable the new bridge to be built had to cross the land on the west side of the High Street.

Work at the bridge went on all the next week while the accounts for 1807-10 and 1810-13 were hurriedly prepared for a meeting on 16 February. There was not enough money in hand to pay for what was being done until, after the meeting, some tenants paid their arrears.

All King's expenses are noted. They include the payments made for travelling through the Turnpike Gates, watching the gap, and for the materials and the work which went on through February and into March. In April King had to attend the Quarter Sessions at Maidstone to, in his words 'Indict the bridge'; that is to present the bridge as being in want of repair. The chaise and expenses came to £1 13s and the Constable who went with him, with his expenses, another 7s 6d.

King acted with vigour as Negotiator, Engineer, and Contractor for the provision of the vital temporary footbridge. His bill covered the major part of the work, but he did not charge the usual 2½ per cent for supervision or measuring, nor for his time negotiating with Mr Willard at Sevenoaks, nor for his attendance before the magistrates. Later, when he worked on the bridge himself, he did charge at the rate of six shillings a day.

The Wardens' papers are silent as to why King, wearing several hats, should have been chosen to 'present' the broken bridge to the County. The situation was complicated. As we have seen, the Wardens were charged with the duty of expending the profits of the lands on the repair of the lesser bridges, but that did not relieve the County of its responsibility for the bridges, and indeed, under the 1530 Statute of Bridges, for a hundred yards of highway on each side of each bridge (a point which was made successfully in the case of Pen Bridge, Higham Lane in the 1950s).

It was fortunate for the town and County that John King was a Warden; he appears as a Builder, Architect and Surveyor, and a man knowledgeable, enterprising and vigorous in all his undertakings. He was well respected and likely to get on with the work and sort out any difficulties later. Few Wardens would have had the knowledge to act as he did, and been able to spend so much time away from their normal occupations.

The County in preparing to build a new bridge proposed to remove the hump back by raising the road gradually on brick flood arches. The accounts contain an item for calling a Towns Meeting at which it was agreed the Wardens' funds could be spent on such arches. However the County built the new single span arch bridge (about 25 feet wide) without the flood arches. The County then commissioned and sent to the Wardens a somewhat muddled report setting out major and minor repairs required to the northern bridges.

Dipping Places. In 1598 the washing place at the Lower Bridge over the main river had been furnished with a stone wall, steps and a platform, all part of the bridge structure and regarded as a necessity by the townsfolk. It is not clear whether the stone platform continued to be protected with a stone wall, but there are many later references to repairs to posts and rails and a timber platform at both the Lower and the Great Bridge. On 26 October 1741, at the Court Leet held at the Rose and Crown, Robert Weller and John Colegate were chosen Town Wardens. They paid for sandstone for the bridges bought from the castle, and 'new makeing the stage at the dipping place'.

In 1765 the Wardens paid the large sum of £22 12s 7d for sawing, cleaving and carpenter's work, for taking the timber from Lodge Oak to the sawpit, and sawing the timber for 'the diping place, the stage, and grates against the river and lower bridge'. The old posts and rails from the lower bridge and river were saved and used on the Town Lands.

The Great Bridge was rebuilt by the County in 1774-75 on the old foundations. Local craftsmen were employed altering houses to make room for a temporary bridge. To ease the steep gradient of the old bridge the approaches were raised which made the newly paved way down to the dipping place and the horsewash much steeper.

From April 1791 when France declared war on the continental countries of Europe there was ferment in England, but in Tonbridge there was other trouble. At the Court Leet held for the Manor of Tonbridge on the 5th November 1791 it was presented by the Jury:

> that the Horsepond and dipping place by the Great Bridge were out of repair and very dangerous and that a person on horseback having rode into the horsepond about six weeks before had difficulty getting out for want of its repair and the Town Wardens should repir it as they had done so within the knowledge of some of the Jury and they could prove it for near a hundred years and if they dont do it within six months they be indicted at the Quarter Sessions or Assizes.

Presentment at Quarter Sessions was to be avoided, not only for the odium of alleged neglect, but because of the legal expenses involved. As ordered, the Constable 'presented' the horsepond at the Quarter Sessions of Midsummer 1792 and the Parish of Tonbridge (not the Wardens) was indicted. At the Michaelmas Sessions Mr Hooker, as Surveyor, pleaded not guilty. Scoones, the lawyers, instructed Mr John Bailey of Counsel to move at the hearing 'that the Indictment be quashed' on the grounds of misinformation that the Parish was liable to repair. Counsel's fee which was a guinea was magnanimously paid by the Wardens:

> At the next Court Leet the matter was brought into Question again and was debated upon which the Town Wardens undertook to repair the place, being satisfied that the Parish was not obliged to do so and it is now [1793] undergoing repair. It should seem that neither the one nor the other ought to repair and that the want of it was not Indictable. Epiphany 1793. 33 Geo 3.

The horsewash was neither a highway nor a bridge and therefore was neither the responsibility of the Parish nor the County; but nor was it the responsibility of the Wardens. They had maintained it and the dipping place, but were in a cleft stick. They could easily refute responsibility by producing the document from which they derived their powers, but few of the works they paid for were legally authorised, and a glance at the 'ancient writings' would expose them once again to the charge that they had regularly misemployed the profits from the lands. It is little wonder that in the previous century the Court found that 'the ancient writings' had been 'concealed if not suppressed by some of the said Wardens or by some of the Inhabitants'.

In the event the Wardens, Edward Thomas Rodmell and James Vine, did repair the horsewash. They also bought a chain from Mr Hooker for £1 4s and put up posts and staples and made all safe and resumed maintenance of the area.

The Clappers. The Clappers were important and the Wardens always acted quickly when they were damaged. Described as 'bridges of wood' the walkways were thick slabs of oak from the Town Lands, raised several feet above the ground on heavy piles and stout trestles – some had handrails. The joints were reinforced with iron plates as large as eighteen inches by six, and 'dogs' were used to secure the timbers together. ('Dogs' are square iron bars, shaped like goalposts; the ends are sharpened to drive them into the timbers which are to be held together.)

In 1625 there is a reference to 'all the clappers between the bridges'. In 1634 (when identification was not helped by the Great Bridge being described as 'the fifth, alias the first') the ground between the bridges was described as deep and hollow and many witnesses confirmed that without the clappers neither man nor beast could traverse the road in winter or in times of flood. One site only is spoken of and could have been either a 40 yard stretch south of the Great Bridge or north of the Lower Bridge. In 1719 there is an entry for mending the clappers and the same hand has added 'at the Great Bridge' suggesting there was at least one other set. In bills from 1776 to 1810 the length between the Great Bridge and the Loggerheads bridge could be 'Clapper Street', while in another the clappers appear to be south of the Loggerheads Bridge. Mr Woodgate in his will of 1786 left 'Clapper fields east side of Clapper Street in Tonbridge Town to sister Anne Woodgate for life then to nephew William Woodgate' and a meadow near the Lower Bridge where King wanted to put his temporary bridge in 1814 was called 'Clapper Mead'. To further confuse the question of the clappers, Dumbreck has a note that at the Court Leet in 1703 it was ordered 'That the clapper between the two Lower Bridges to be repaired by the shop to whom it belongs'. The evidence suggests there were several sets of clappers, some privately owned. It may be that as the low land was built on, the flood water was diverted and new clappers had to be made.

In 1752 for the first time the dipping place and clappers were recorded as having been repaired with yellow deal, probably brought up the river by a Medway Company barge. In May 1768 John Burges was paid for 'puting Down the posts the Ice had Taken up' and 'master upperton for help and Beer Setling down the portel the ice had taken up'.

Other works
In the terms of the 1601 Act, which was the basis of the law of charities, all the Town Lands' profits but for the money spent on the lower bridges and the narrow strip between Church Lane and the Market Cross was 'misemployed'. In addition to spending money on the paving, the clappers and the dipping places, the Wardens cleared stones from the river, paved across the rough muddy road from Church Lane to Bank Street, and Swan Lane to the Market Cross, and recovered from the water the ornaments off the bridge. Despite what Lambarde and Neve say about their keeping clean the town, they spent nothing on regular scavenging. On the contrary the roads were filthy and the Manor rolls are constantly referring to dung and offal obstructing the pavements.

There is no doubt the Wardens interpreted their powers freely for the good of the town, and on 23 April 1793 there is the first mention of a new, expensive, and equally unauthorised venture. The Wardens paid Mr Mercer and Mr Thomas King £2.1.2 for 'Allowance when working at the Pump and Dipping Place.'

There was no piped water supply in Tonbridge. Outside the town there was a public spring and well at Dry Hill. Within the town there were private wells, a dipping place at the bottom of the Slade, and a public well at the bottom of Castle Street. The flow of water at the High Street dipping places depended on the management of weirs. The Mill stream was penned, and in summer, and more frequently after the river was made navigable, there was little flow at the Great Bridge, and at the little bridge there could be no flow at all.

In this Wardenship for the first time a pump was provided. Many local tradesmen were involved and the pump acquired a personality of its own. Sandstone was cut from Mr Ollive's quarry and squared; paving was laid; oak elm and other timber was bought and jointed for slabs and rails; a turned wooden ball and a bucket sucker were made; there was iron for the barrel, the rods, the keys, the ends of the planks, and 'the grate for the end of its trunk', and a long stay and hoop 'for the end of its nose'; there were 'bail and burs for the under sucker', leather and tallow for the 'sucker', and washers, iron and wood for the handle.

The pump was regarded as vulnerable. It was fitted with a chain and staple, and a hasp which weighed 7½ lb, and it was padlocked. Finally, on 31 July 1793 it was erected at the dipping place beside the Great Bridge and painted. Items in bills referring to the first pump come to over £30 and thereafter expenses which appear to be connected with repairing it bring the cost to at least £69 during its first twelve years.

The Georgian Wardens made at least one other contribution to public welfare. When the Great Bridge was rebuilt, Mr Wise had been paid by the County for lighting, and when paving was going on there is a payment by the Wardens for 'watching the stones'; otherwise there were no public street lamps in the town.

On 19 August and 2 September 1823 when so much York paving was being laid, three large lanthorns were bought together with candles for them. The lamps did not last long; on 3 and 5 September they had been damaged and had to be repaired, and new tin rims were provided and fitted to the lamp irons. In the same months there are again items for watching; the watchers were paid 1s 6d a night each; candles cost 7s 0d for 12 lb, and oil 10d a time for an unknown quantity. It has been written that this experiment went on for a few months, but although there is a single reference to a 'lamp post' there are no more recorded payments for lighting until the coming of gas in Queen Victoria's days.

There can be no doubt the streets were dangerous after dark, not only from the uneven pavings, but from other trips. As early as 1716 the Manor court ordered 'No person to fix their pens in the town till Market Day in the morning that the same may be no annoyance to persons walking the night before'.

In the 1825-28 term the Wardens again broke new ground. They shared with Mr Kipping, the Surveyor of Highways, the £7 purchase price paid to 'John Snelling for Ground at bottom of the Town'. Presumably the land was for road widening.

There was one less happy way in which money went. When the Prince Regent became George IV in 1820, John Luckhurst a Leather Cutter and James Arrow had been Wardens for two months. The account book having been abandoned, their 1819-22 Accounts are the first in the new book of the new reign. The Wardens and Scoones the lawyer spent a great deal of time and money over the problems they had inherited. Mr Town had been the only active Warden and it was difficult to get from him any papers, books, leases or accounts and Mr Ashdown of Mr Scoones office, who appears to have acted as a Receiver, had, through the bankruptcies of tenants become the notional tenant of some of the Town Lands and had re-let them. Luckhurst and Arrow had difficulty getting in money from the tenants and received none of the £400 due from the previous Wardens. A later Warden calculated that from 1819 to October 1823 the losses sustained by the Funds of The Town Wardens was £516 8s 2d.

Throughout Georgian times there was a gradual increase in the fees paid for preparing the accounts, and in addition to the new items of payment of interest to Beechings Bank, the legal fees for every step of letting and leasing the lands increased.

Out of the Georgian Age

There was little change in the day to day work of the Wardens as the Georgian Age closed; they cleared snow, paid unemployed bargemen for breaking the ice, and paid for the prosecution of a felon for stealing 'the case of the cock' and the plug of the pump.

In the summer of 1832 it was not only the passing of the Reform Bill that excited the townsfolk of Tonbridge; some were equally excited over the question of the Wardens' 'ancient pavements'. From being 'notable' as refinements they had become in the eyes of some, 'notorious'. The bridges had been macadamised a few years before, and the Highway Surveyor and Turnpike Trustees had surfaced their roads in the same way. The Wardens' strip from the Market Cross to the Church Lane seems to have still remained 'paved' and rough. After a great deal of heavy handed decision making (see Appendix 5) in King's words:

> Sept. The pavements in the middle of the Town of Tonbridge taken up and the Road Macadamized in ten days – it extended from Church lane to the Chequers Inn and King & Brown Superintendents. Town Wardens were Richd. Martin Austen, grocer and Wm. Brown Architect

The Highway Surveyor made a contribution for his part of the work and in the same month William Chalklin was paid £26 7s 5d for:

> Taking up the rough stone Pavements in the High Street from the Chequers to the Church Lane and paving a water channel on each side of the McAdamized Road.

In October he received £66 1s 2½d for:

> Taking up part of the Rough Stone Pavement between the Water Channel and the Footpath on each side of the High Street and also part of the same footpaths and Repaving the whole.

To maintain the new heavily cambered surfaces the Wardens had regularly to pay for scraping the loose surface to shape, filling pot holes, and for watering to keep the binding slurry from drying out and blowing away. In 1833 two patent water carts were bought to do the work. The Trustees of the Tonbridge Turnpike Roads paid for one cart, and the Wardens for the other. Each cost £29 and thereafter the Wardens paid for the repair of their cart and the fittings, and for regularly greasing and housing it. In time the 'Tonbridge thread' hose connections had to be adapted to the new Whitworth standards.

The Wardens also repaved the bridges and many footpaths and until 1836 were re-paving above the Great Bridge. York stone slabs were laid against the houses; the work involved levelling the ground and in some cases underpinning the front walls. In front of the Rose and Crown clinkers were laid (perhaps where the coaches crossed the footway). Named owners of houses and the Highway Surveyor paid their 'apportioned part' of the cost of the works.

Although there was no waste water from a piped supply, there were places in the upper town where short private 'sewers' under the paths discharged rain water and slops on to the edge of the carriage-way. Maintaining a tight surface on the macadamised roads needed water, but too much water destroyed the new surface and therefore had to be removed as quickly as possible. That was the next task facing the Wardens. On 31 August 1837 William Chalklin agreed to:

> ... do all the bricklayers' work in forming a main drain from near the Great Bridge to the northern end of the Terrace according to the Specifications and to make good all the present drains for the Sum of One Hundred and Sixteen Pounds.

The Terrace was south of the Elephant and Castle, and the work was put in hand and paid for in instalments. Many of the householders' small 'sewers' must have been connected up as the total cost was at least £174 and in September and October 14 householders paid the Wardens £125 as their contribution to the work.

With the settling of the bills for the main Drain the Wardens brought the finishing touches to the works they had undertaken in the Georgian Age, and in the first winter of Victoria's reign, although the eight o'clock curfew was still tolled from the Church tower, they marked the new era by lighting the streets with gas on the moonless nights of the month.

Sequels

The broken bridge. Accounts for the Wardenship of John King and William Town for the term 1813-16 and 1816-17 do not balance; they were not signed, and cash which should have been brought forward does not appear.

On 20 May 1817 is recorded the receipt of the first of four payments of 'Dividends from assigns of Mr. John King'; in all they total £90 11s 4d, a figure very close to a recently calculated balance of £91 17s 8d due from him but not brought into the accounts at the time.

In 1822 Mr Ashdown, after vain attempts to obtain all the information he needed, prepared a set of accounts for 1816-19 for Town alone; his fellow Warden, Parker does not appear. The accounts were agreed and signed on 6 February. The amount brought forward is slightly different from the balance shown as in hand. At the end of the term there should have been £440 12s 6d to pass on, but that sum was never brought into any surviving accounts. There are no more entries, the next pages of the account book have been carefully cut out, and the book was abandoned though only half filled.

What happened is obscure, but an item in a later bill of Scoones is for:

> Sept. 1816. Preparing Proof of Debt under Mr. John King's Commission and attend Mr. Town swearing the same and duty   6s. 8d.

(The 1866 report on the Charities in Tonbridge observed that at this period 'about £440 appears to have been lost to this Charity, and the account-book mutilated'. The mutilation leaves intact the record of receipts of some rents in these years. In rebuilding the Lower Bridge the County did not build the flood arches; the Wardens therefore did not have to pay for them as authorised by the Magistrates and Inhabitants of the Town.)

The first account in the new book was approved at the Court Leet held on 6 November 1822 with the not-surprising comment in William Jewhurst's handwriting: 'The Jury after inspecting and approving the foregoing accounts recommend that in future they be made up and submitted to the Jury Annually'. (Mr John King who appears elsewhere as hard working and conscientious was probably bankrupted through the bank failure, but made good the deficiencies in his own accounts, and recovered his position. He carried out the 1820 enlargement of the Parish Church, the construction of The Terrace and Rose Place opposite, and many other works. He was well respected and later acted for the Town Wardens. He died in 1837. His yard was off Kinnings Row, behind The Terrace and what is now Minerva House in Bordyke, and remained a builders yard until the 1960s.)

The other bridges. At the end of the nineteenth century the lower High Street was widened, and the three middle streams were culverted. The only signs of the northern or Loggerheads Bridge are some manhole covers in the footway and the narrow shops (Nos 83 and 85) which were built over the old stream bed. The Loggerheads had been on the opposite side of the road (No. 94) and when it was rebuilt in the widening, the stone from the old bridge, recording its repair by the County in 1628 was built into the front wall. It bore the initials 'W H' and a carved heart. (In 1574 William Harte and Thomas Johnson had been the Wardens who enfeoffed their successors with the town lands). When the new Post Office was built after the first World War the stone was removed to the castle where it was cherished until smashed to steady a barrow run in 1987.

There is nothing to mark the next Bridge but a pipe discharging into the stream at the end of Botany.

A stone in the wall of No. 53, on the east side of the High Street, marks the site of Osborne's Bridge over 'the back stream of the river' and commemorates its repair by the County in 1630. It bears the same initials and heart as the 1628 stone. In 1872 the Lower Bridge was rebuilt by the County.

The Clappers. There is nothing in the Wardens' documents to mark the last of the clappers. Work was done to them in 1817, well after the Lower Bridge had been rebuilt. By 1841, many of the meadows fronting the highway had been built on, and the old style clappers would have blocked the access to the new premises.

The Pump. At an unknown date the Wardens fixed a second pump at the Lower Bridge, and in 1846 or 47 moved the first one from the horsewash to the Town Hall. As a direct result of shouldering the responsibility of providing those public sources of water, they continued for over a hundred years to foot the bill for the mains water to the drinking fountains which succeeded their pumps.

Conclusion

The books of accounts set out the works of the Wardens through years of ever-changing needs, standards and resources. They are not only an invaluable record of tenants, rents, tradesmen and labourers and the cost and sources of materials, but of the character and personality of Wardens from many walks of life and their attitude to their problems.

The Georgian Wardens of the Town Lands of Tonbridge worked hard for the benefit of the town they knew so well. They responded quickly and effectively to crises, and to new and changing conditions economically, and with minimum bureaucracy, because they understood the needs of the townsfolk to whom they felt responsible. From time to time a meticulous Warden, parish clerk or scrivener tried to make sure the law and procedures were obeyed, but generally such niceties were not allowed to interfere with the consensus of what was needful for the good of the town.

The Georgian Wardens had cared for their town from the age of the quill pen, when coaches could not travel in winter, through the amazing transformation made by the canalisation of the river to the threshold of the age of swift smooth travel by railway, and as their predecessors had done they faithfully, but pragmatically, followed the spirit of the intentions of their Elizabethan forbears. In Victorian times, when the coming of the railway led to the appalling sanitary conditions in the lower part of the town the Victorian Wardens, in the same enlightened spirit, paid for the printing and distribution of advice in cholera epidemics and for lime to disinfect the sewers and ditches. They also paid for an Inspector to report on conditions in the town.

The town has reason to remember and be grateful to the unknown original donors of the lands and to the Wardens of the Town Lands for all their Works.

Sources

Items belonging to the present Town Wardens: four surviving books, some bills and dockets, correspondence, and copies of other documents – see Appendix 1.

Tonbridge Reference Library: John King's Notes, The Dumbreck Papers, Tonbridge Notebooks and Card Index (TU12/ Z10-11)

Centre for Kentish Studies: Gordon Ward Collection (U442 Q7 – for inquisition of 1634)

Wadmore, B, *Some Details in the History of the Parish of Tonbridge* (Tonbridge, 1906 – for churchwardens)

British Library: Extracts from parish and assize records in British Library, and copy of part of the account for rebuilding the Great Bridge, provided by Dr C W Chalklin

Appendix 1: *A note on the surviving Wardens' records*

The first account book runs from 1571 to 1760. It notes the election of the Wardens, the names of their tenants and the rents. No pattern is followed in setting out income and expenditure. The handwriting varies from almost illegible scrawl to beautiful calligraphy. There are gaps in the entries and some pages have been neatly cut out. The book was always examined and signed by the succeeding Wardens and others present at the passing of the accounts.

The second book runs from 1759 to 1819 with little information on elections and lettings; many entries are 'As per Bill'. The book was abandoned when only half full.

The third book runs from 1822 to 1911 and is a magnificent leather volume, lined and ruled, and professionally written. The quality of the information varies; a Minute Book from 1859 to 1950 complements some entries.

Taken together the books give a broad picture of the Wardens' work, but from 1745, some vouchers, dockets and bills survive, and give the names of the men and boys who did the work, what they were paid, where they worked, from where and from whom materials were obtained, and at what price. The spelling is variable and in many dockets and bills is phonetic; when read aloud the accents of the writers are heard.

Some of the gaps in the accounts were left at the time; others were made later, usually for unhappy reasons, and the records cannot therefore form the basis of a structured analysis of the Wardens' work. The whole archive is a lucky dip from which every prize throws a light on the changes in the town through the Georgian age and to the opening of the new world of Victoria.

The Town Lands were known as such in 1431 and there had been records before the first book was started, but by 1598 the books were in a muddle and in that year the two serving Wardens, 'wyth the consent of diverse of the chiefs of the [the word 'Parish' deleted] Towne of Tunbredge', bought a new book and paid the Vicar, the Revd John Stockwood, to go through the old accounts and write them up afresh – see the illustration on p. 82 above.

The Vicar was paid 3s 4d for his labours and rewrote the books from 1571. Thereafter successive scribes continued to record in ever-changing styles of handwriting and detail, the works and misadventures of the Wardens. The deletion of the word 'Parish' in the first book is important, and until 1974 it remained a tenet of this Charity that the choice of Wardens and the profits from the lands were matters solely for the 'Towne' and not the 'Parish'.

The entries in documents vary from a bald fact to a fully detailed description. The documents of which copies survive include the Indenture, The Decree, and reports on the bridges.

Appendix 2: Wages

The wages paid to craftsmen and others are taken from the Town Wardens' account books, and after 1745 are supplemented from bills or dockets supporting the accounts. The rate is given here in pence by the day of an unknown number of hours, unless otherwise stated. There are gaps in continuity because in some periods entries are for measured work, and in some cases for other reasons the daily wage rates cannot be ascertained.

Beer, because the ingredients had been boiled and it was nutritious, was a safe, healthy and important item of diet. The beer allowance does not follow a regular pattern, and in some cases where it is not entered on a bill for labour, there is a separate bill from an innkeeper for 'Beer for the paviours' or something similar which may or may not be associated with the particular labour item. There is no evidence of the changes in the cost per quart.

The earlier part of the table illustrates the steadiness of a craftsman's wage before Georgian times.

Date	Crafts-man	Lab-ourer		Notes
1665	24d	12d		The beer allowance was 1d a day
		8d	(boy)	for each man and boy.
1695		12d		Casual labour, spreading stones
1702	24d	18d		Beer money 6d for 9 men/days
1708				Beer only recorded
1718	24d			The master man and two 'servants'
				hewing timber all received this rate.
1723		16d		Work and status not stated
1753	24d	14d		Two bricklayers with one labourer,
				plus 1d a day beer money each .
	24d			Carpenter
1759		14d		Boy spreading stones.
1768	48d for horse and cart and man; plus 2d a day for beer			
1772	24d	14d		Paving. Each allowed 2d a day
		10d		beer money.
	24d			Carpenter. Beer money added.
1773-4	24d	18d		Paving. Each allowed 2d a day
		14d		beer money.
		10d		[Through the years named boys
		8d		climbed the wages ladder.]
		6d	(boy)	
		12d		Unspecified work. Casual labourer

The Work of the Town Wardens

Date	Crafts-man	Lab-ourer		Notes
1776	50p			Horse and cart and man and beer
1785	24d	18d		Paving. Plus beer 2d a day each
	72d A cart and 2 horses a day. No mention of man			
1786	24d			Carpenter. Plus 2d a day beer
	24d	18d		Bricklaying at bridge
		10d	(boy)	This seems to be the same
		8d	(boy)	boy.
1798				8 pots of beer 40d
1802	36d			Oak piles to bridge. The man was a master carpenter [builder] himself.
		24d		Labourer; unknown work
1802	36d	22d		Paving. In this group there are two
		18d		craftsmen and two lower paid men. The master man and his boy work together at 60d the pair. The next year when working alone the master is paid 42d.
1803	40d			Probably a carpenter
1804	42d			Bricklayer
1805	40d			Carpenter
				Paving? 5d a day beer per man
1807	60d			The master builder himself
	50d			His craftsman
1808-10	52d			The master paviour or bricklayer
	50d			himself, and two other paviours
		42d		A paviour's man
		20d		A paviour's man
		12d	(boy)	
1814	48d – 72d in steps of 6d.			The master carpenter and his skilled men on the broken bridge. An emergency in which work went on in icy conditions and at weekends.
1816	48d	36d		Bricklayer and labourers. Some of
		30d		this year's rates are inclusive of beer at 3d a day.
1817	44d			Master bricklayer
	42d			Bricklayer

Date	Crafts-man	Lab-ourer		Notes
1817		28d		Labourer. The beer allowance is charged at 6d a day per man.
	48d	36d		Bricklaying
		30d		Breaking stones
		24d		5 weeks @ 12 shillings a week
		16d		2 weeks @ 8 shillings a week
		6d		1 week @ 3 shillings a week
		18d		9 nights watching; 13s 6d
		?		11 nights 19s
		?		9 nights 11s
		24d		8 nights @ 2s a night
1818	42d	8d	(boy)	Paving. Masterman and craftsman
1820	42d			Paviour/Bricklayer. Masterman
	40d	27d		All plus 3d a day ''Lowance'

On a single occasion, 120d a day plus 24d for beer was charged for the masterman and his labourer. The beer allowances are erratic.

Date	Crafts-man	Lab-ourer		Notes
1822	54d			Painting
1823	70d			a day was charged for a bricklayer and his labourer
1825	78d			a day was charged for a bricklayer and his labourer
1827	62d			plus 8d tool money, mason working circular granite
1828		21d		Breaking stones
1830	40d			a day each for men fencing.
1832		24d		Scraping the road. Casual labour
	52d			The masterman paving.
	48d	36d)		The others. Taking up and
		30d)		relaying paving – repairing
		24d)		bridges.
	60d			Mason. Laying York stone and steps.

78d a day for a horse and cart - no man mentioned

 96d & 102d for horses and carts – no man mentioned.

Date	Crafts-man	Lab-ourer		Notes
1835-7		30d		Casual labour; sifting or raking stones.

Appendix 3: Accounts

Items from the accounts of John Brookshead and George Sherlock (1717-20) when the collapse of the South Sea Bubble was causing distress to some Tonbridge townsfolk.

1719	£. s. d
payed to Mr Dorman for the half of seven load of grett stone	1:04:06
payed Mrs Jefraye for 10 Load of Stons for the briges	0:10:00
payed to John Pares for Carieg of stones	1:10:00
payed to Will Beates for 19 Loads of gravfiells	1:02:02
payed to Mr Johnson for bere and bread	7:10
payed to Will Dutson for worcke and pavfinge	4:12:03
payed to John Broocksted for worke and Lime	2:19:08½
paid Edwd Hilman & Wm Curd for 2 days & 1/2 work felling & flawing of Timber	0:09:02
pd Jacob Mercer for amending the pavemt.	1:01:00
For my owne work 2 days & 1/2	0:05:00
2 Servts. working 3 days hewing of Timber & other work	12:00
For my owne work 3 days about the 3d bridge	0:06:00
for 2 Servants working 4 days apeecs	0:16:00
pd Coppins Man for drawing Timber out of the Lane to the bridge	0:00:06
2 Servts. work one day att the lower bridge Spurring up a post & setting up a post & rail at the Steps	0:04:00
pd for beer & bread to the Carryers of the Stones to the bridges	0:03:06
pd for Sawing	1:09:08
3 Servts work 2 days & 1/2 posting & railing in Wrights Land	0:12:06
pd Jacob Mercer for work about the bridges & paving	6:03:06
2 mens worke 2 days about the Clappers & a footbridge in Mr. Vanderlure's feild	0:08:00
for 2 peeces of Slabbs & nails used about the Clappers	06
pd for bread & drink for Dorman & the Stone Carrier	0:02:04
pd for drink at putting up the Timber work att the Bridge	0:02:06
for my Servts felling of a pollard for a post and hanging the Gate & mending another Gate & other work	0:04:00
for a Stout Gate in Mr Vanderlure his Land	0:09:00
& a Stout hanging post	0:02:06
One Rail	0:00:08

One days work hanging the gate & mending the Clappers
att the Great Bridge   0:04:00
Carrying the Gate & post & rail   0:01:00
One days work trying up the planks & Slabbs   0:02:00
pd for carrying Tymber from the Towne Lands to
the bridges   0:06:00
pd for drink for John Parris the Carryer of the Tymber etc   0:01:03

Appendix 4: The expenditure

The information in the documents varies from good to nil; consequently the following pattern is crude. An '★' indicates some work was or may have been done. A '?' indicates a doubt about the accuracy of the allocation. Brackets indicate a 'minus quantity'. There is not always a distinction between structural work to a bridge and paving over it; such work is often tied to work to the 'Dipping places and horsewash'. 'P' is work to the pump. 'Other' includes legal fees, work on the town lands, and refreshment on any occasion. 'Rmns' is the money which should have been passed on to the next Wardens. The figures denote £s.

Term	Cash available	Pavings	Bridges	Clappers	Other	Rmns
1711–14	63	36	3	7	nil	17
1714–17	70	59	0	0	26	(15)
1717–20	56	26	11	1	4	14
1720–23	80	60	★	★	19	1
1723–26	64	52	3	8	1	8
1726–29	72	50?	7	2	3	10
1729–32	74	46	★	1	23	4
1732–35	71	30	0	0	4	37
1735–38	109	101	2	4	2	0
1738 41	71	58	2	3	6	2
1741–44	73	49	3	3	3	15
1744–47	87	83	1	1	1	1
1747–50	146	87	11	★	11	37
1750–53	128	114	11	1	0	2
1753–56	95	77	2	★	12	4
1756–59	91	92	★	1	2	(4)
1759–62	86	54	2	7	7	16
1762–65	101	86	11	3	0	1
1765–68	112	43	39	2	7	21
1768–71	131	104	2	7	1	17
1771–74	123	45	12	2	★	64
1774–77	173	159	11	★	1	2
1777–80	107	59	1	1	2	44
1780–83	209	109	55	14	2	29
1783–86	164	87	99	0	5	(27)

Term	Cash available	Pavings	Bridges		Clappers	Other	Rmns
1786-89	133	52	4		6	28	43
1789-92	171	113	2		0	7	49
1792-95	174	103	0	44P	0	7	49
1795-98	183	22	1	5P	2	13	140
1798-1801	328	208	30	17P	2	66	5
1801-04	197	163	11	3P	0	5	15
1804-07	186	136	32		0	5	13
1807-10	140	112	12		33	18	(35)
1810-13	535	?	?	4P	?	?	158
1813-16	<— — — 374 — — —>						88!
1816-19	175	51	accounts not approved			4	120
1819-22	333	251	19		3	12	48
1822-25	363	243	13		2	47	58
1825-27)	108	48	0		0	1	59
1827-28)	246	121	★		0	15	110
1828-31	319	59	4		0	19	237
1831-34	472	324	27	16P	0	21	84
1834-37	536	235	11	13P	176	27	
			(snow)		(main drain)		

Appendix 5: Documents concerning the macadamising of the Wardens' part of the High Street in 1832

The question of whether the Wardens should macadamise the strip of the High Street on which they could legally spend their profits, roused much feeling, and, ever mindful of the need to carry the townsfolk with them in any decisions they made, the Wardens called a meeting of the inhabitants, advertised by 100 bills printed for them by Fanny Daken. In preparation for the meeting, the accounts for many earlier years were scrutinised and calculations were made about past costs and of providing various types of surface. The items which follow are from the Wardens' papers; the newspapers have not been consulted.

1   From John King's Notebook

1832 September. The pavement in the middle of the Town of Tonbridge taken up and the ROAD MacAdamized in ten days – it extended from Church Lane to the Chequers Inn and King & Brown Superintendents. Town Wardens were Richard Martin Austen, grocer and William Brown Architect. [Brown was King's partner and a Warden.]

2   The Notice

The WARDENS of the TUNBRIDGE TOWN LANDS, respectfully request the Inhabitants of the TOWN OF TUNBRIDGE to attend a MEETING at the COURT HALL, on THURSDAY, the 23rd instant, at 3 o'Clock, for the purpose of taking into consideration the propriety of RE-PAVING the HIGH Street of the said Town, from the Court Hall to the Church Lane, or of taking up the present Pavement, and forming a McADAMIZ'D ROAD

Tunbridge, 17 AUGUST, 1832

DAKENS, PRINTER & BOOKBINDER, TUNBRIDGE

3   Letter from the Revd Thomas Knox D.D. (Headmaster of Tonbridge School), 19 August 1832

To Mr. Brown, Architect, Tonbridge.   Paid

Sir,
    I have received a Notice of Meeting on the 23rd on the subject of the Pavements in the Town. I shall feel very much obliged to you to

acquaint me at whose instigation this meeting is holden and what probability there is of succeeding in removing the Nuisance.

Do you think it would be worth while for me to attend? If the hour of Meeting could be changed to one oclock, I could run up by the early Hastings Coach and return at four – but I do not think that I can spare two days.

I saw Mr. Jewhurst here this morning – who expressed his decided opinion for the Removal of the pavements – but he will not be able to attend. Let me hear from you by return of Post.

Hastings   Yours etc   Thomas Knox.

Aug 19 1832

I am writing this in the dark. If the Tonbridge Tradesmen were to hear all that I do against the Pavements, they would not suffer such a Disgrace to attach to the place – Provision must be made for Watering the whole road.

4   Letter from William Brown (Warden) to Thomas Knox at Hastings, 20 August 1832

20th August 1832

The Meeting on the 23rd inst. is called by the Wardens of the Tonbridge Town Lands for the express purpose of ascertaining the opinion of the Inhabitants as to the paving or macadamizing the Town – and by this opinion it is the present intention of the Wardens to adhere so far as they have the power and means to carry the same into effect – The Wardens wish every Inhabitant to attend the Meeting that the Business may be fairly and deliberately considered so that blame may not attach to them by acting in accordance with the opinion of the Meeting

I am Sir
Your Obt. Svt
Wm. Brown

Thos. J. Knox D.D.

5   Letter from proprieters and drivers of coaches, vans, etc, undated

To the Inhabitants of the town of Tunbridge.

We the undersigned proprietors & Drivers of the Several Coaches Vans, Waggons etc. etc. which have to pass through the town of Tunbridge, do earnestly solicit the Inhabitants of the said town to cause the pavement now existing in the High street to be removed.

We hereby attest that if so required, we could adduce evidence of great and serious injury, sustained by us, in the Conveyance of goods, passengers etc., over the said pavements and we farther attest that in our Knowledge and experience of several parts of the Kingdom, no instance has occurred in which the removal of ancient pavements has not given great satisfaction to the resident Inhabitants as to the travelling Public.

Robert Gray	Thos. Benett	Thos. Wilkinson
Thos. Wickham	J.P.Hart	James Borads(?)
Edward Eastland	John Stephens(?)	Joseph Noakes
R. T. Horne	Edward Pawley	[some signatures doubtful]

6   Letter from tradesmen in Hastings (undated)

To the Inhabitants of the Town of Tunbridge.

We the undersigned Tradesmen in the Town of Hastings, hereby attest, that we have experienced no injury or inconvenience whatever in our several Trades by the removal of the Pavement in High Street, and other places:- but that, on the contrary, we consider ourselves benefited and the public convenience and comfort promoted by adoption of the System of Mr. McAdam-

Convinced by the experience of some years of the great advantages of gravelled Roads, particularly in places of great thoroughfare, we do strongly recommend the Inhabitants of Tunbridge to remove from their High Street, that pavement which has long formed the subject of general complaint – and which must be as great a nuisance to the Inhabitants as it is to the Public. 19 signatures.

Hugh Penfold, Ironmonger;	Henry Williams, Jeweller;
William Hill, Hatter;	Sam Duke, Breeches Maker;
George Bennett, Draper;	John Smith, Baker;
H. N. Williams, Wine Merchant;	J. Waghorne, Butcher;
G & A Jackson, Drapers;	S. Foster, Taylor;
J? Amoone?, Mercer;	Wm. Bayley, Stationer;
Richard Weston, Watchmaker;	H. Lea, Druggist;
Henry Dunk, Grocer;	G. Wooll, Stationer;
Saml. Roberts, Shoemaker;	Jos. Brown, Penmaker;
Mrs. Powell, Librarian.	

[One wonders why Dr Knox's tradesmen had such an interest in Tonbridge pavements. Were they paved with gold? A respected Schoolmaster did not, it appears, have any carriers, carters, builders, fishmongers, millers or oilmen among his acquaintances]

7 Calculation of expenses

23 Aug.   Calculation of the expenses of following different pavements and of forming one macadamized road in the the High Street of Tonbridge Town from opposite the Town Hall to the Church Lane, being a distance of 135 yards and average width 9 yards.

All to take up and relay with:-

1. Aberdeen 9" cubes	£1082
2. paving centre 6 yards Aberdeen 9" cubes with Rag 9" cubes each side	£908
3. 6 yards centre Aberdeen 9" cubes and present rag pavements each side	£740
4. Take up present and repave with same materials	£86
5. Take up present & repave with macadamized Road	£88
Annual expense of keeping same in repair by a 4" coat of Stones every 2 years	£27

8 Summary of expenditure on pavements 1823-31

[This was prepared for the meeting and gives names and amounts of bills by the year; there is a similar analysis of materials]

Town Hall to Church Lane.

1823	£250. 0. 0	1828	£0. 7. 6	
1824	22. 0. 0	1829	30.16. 1	
1825	55. 0. 0	1830	12. 3. 8	(all items listed)
1826	19.18. 0	1831	7. 6	
1827	84.10. 1		Total £475. 2.10	
			Average £59. 7.10d	

9 Minutes of Meeting on 23 August 1832, written by John Scoones in his own hand

Minutes

At a Meeting of the Inhabitants of Tonbridge at the Court Hall on Thursday the 23rd August 1832 Convened for the purpose of taking into Consideration the propriety of Re-paving the High Street of the said Town from the Court Hall to the Church Lane or of taking up the present pavement and forming a McAdamized Road

PRESENT

Mr. John Scoones Chairman
Revd. Dr. Knox represented by John Carnell

Messrs.

Stephen Tinley	Thos. Beeching the younger
Asher Barcham	William Burren
Peter Brown	Thomas Roberts
Leison Prince	William Ware
John Evenden	Thomas Turner
Thomas Jefferson	Bennett
Charles Guest	John Children
William Parker	James Richardson
William Ash	Thomas Kipping

[Some names are doubtful]

Richard Martin Austen)   Wardens.
    William Brown)

Resolved: that a respectful application be made to the Surveyor of the Highways for the Town that he would permit the Wardens of the Town Lands to apply any disposable Surplus in their hands in the formation of a McAdamized Road in that part of the Carriageway of the Town which is at present paved.

Resolved that in support of such application to the Surveyor this Meeting Engages, in the event of the Road being Mcadamized, to join in a Subscription in aid of the Funds of the Town Wardens, towards effectually Watering and continuing the Road Watered throughout the Town

John Scoones
Chairman

10 **Extract from bill sent by Scoones to Wardens**

1834 Nov 1829 Penshurst Coy wish to exchange lands; searching documents for power of Wardens etc.

1832 searching for correspondence with Clerk of the Peace in 1814 preparatory to the meeting of the Inhabitants to consider question of McAdamizing High Street; failing to find evidence of Indictment for Lower Bridge in 1814. Searching for [1576] Fine.   £4. 1. 4

133

The building in Bank Street which from 1726 to 1835 was the Workhouse where poor children received education, and which later became Bank Street School. This drawing by John Stammers shows the building as it was in 1972.

Education in Georgian Tonbridge

Dorothy Stammers

In 1700 the only school in Tonbridge of which there is a reliable record, was the Grammar School (now Tonbridge School) founded by Sir Andrew Judde in 1553. There was no national system of education. Grammar Schools and universities were the monopoly of the Church of England and were mainly nurseries of the Anglican clergy.[1] To be admitted to Tonbridge Grammar School a boy had to be able to write and read in English and Latin. For the poor there was little provision.

Throughout England there were private schools at every level of society which charged fees ranging from several pounds (country boarding schools and academies) to 6d or 2d per week at dame schools[2] – the latter referred to by Dr S J Curtis in his *History of Education in Great Britain* as 'inefficient baby-minding establishments'.

In the eighteenth century it was not a foregone conclusion that poor children should be educated – in fact many eminent gentlemen expressed the opinion that those born to the drudgery of daily labour would, if educated, become discontented and unhappy with their lot. Generally a child who had reached an age at which he or she could be taught, was taught to work. The chimney boy in *The Water Babies* was no fantasy: very young children (often from age seven) were employed doing anything they could conceivably be taught to do.

The earliest record of education for poor children in Tonbridge is of that given by the Workhouse from 1726 when it was built. The children were employed spinning and knitting, spinning what they wore and supplying the House, and also supplying necessitous people outside the House where the Officers judged it necessary. They were also taught to read by such of the women of the House as were

135

capable. Items in Tonbridge Poor Law Books around 1763-71 refer to money paid to various gentlemen for teaching Workhouse children:

Aug. 1763	Sam Crackett	– for his care in teaching the children to read	2/6d
July. 1768	Richard Brooker	– for teaching the children to read	2/6d
Oct. 1768	Henry Chalklin	– do –	2/6d
Oct. 1771	Skinner	– do –	[no amount stated]

It was recorded in 1731 that eight children were put out to apprenticeship and four to the Services. A plea was made, presumably by the Master of the Workhouse, that children should be bound out for a shorter term as they tended to desert their Masters.

In 1698 the Society for Promoting Christian Knowledge (SPCK) was founded and amongst its many aims was the foundation of schools to give a sound education, religious and secular, to the children of the poor. These schools were the Charity Schools, at first in and about London, but soon to spread to all parts of the country. In the 1780s one Robert Raikes sought to revive and expand the facilities of the Sunday School, aiming like the Charity Schools, at rescuing very poor children from vice and ungodliness by instructing them in a curriculum based on the Bible and Catechism.[3] They taught reading and writing and, in some instances, 'summing'. They were mainly supported by Anglican and Methodist clergy.

There is no record of a charity school in Tonbridge at the beginning of the eighteenth century but for Tunbridge Wells SPCK records in 1704-14 refer to 70 poor boys being taught at a Charity School – 67 in summer, 72 in winter. It was supported by contributions made by the nobility and gentry, and collections made at the Chapel door. In 1705 £24 was given to the Master of which £2 was for fuel and the remainder to clothe the boys for the next year. The school was conducted in the ante-gallery of King Charles the Martyr Chapel; in winter, the Chapel being unheated, the school adjourned to a Coffee House. In 1713 the boys were instructed in the three R's by the Chapel Clerk, and later by a Minister. In 1739 Dr Wilson of Tunbridge

Wells advertised for a sober person to teach a Charity School and be Master of a Workhouse. In 1766 there were 50 or more boys and girls being taught by the Clergyman, the school being supported by contributions at the Chapel doors two or three times a year.[4]

In Southborough a school was founded in 1785 by the Executors of the Holmes Trust with income which was more than sufficient for the two schools which the Revd Edward Holmes had founded at Leybourne and East Malling. The school took 32 boys and girls of Tunbridge, 12 of Bidborough and 6 of Speldhurst, recommended by Ministers and Churchwardens of those parishes. In 1819 the income from Holmes' estate was settled between the three schools – £1,050 four-per-cents as endowment to each school. Rents from property in Birling, Ryarsh, Addington, West and East Malling totalling £198 4s 6d were to be divided among the three schools. All the schools had a full complement of scholars, who were taught reading, writing and arithmetic; the masters were Wesleyan Methodists, but the Church Catechism was taught. Each school had its own Trustees, who visited annually when the accounts were audited, the children examined, vacancies filled, and silver pens given to the best writer in each school, as well as Bibles. The salary of the Master was £42, with an additional gratuity of £10 at the July visitation and £14 in October, out of which he provided pens, ink and firing – £7. Children could stay from 7 to 14 years of age, but seldom did.

In Tonbridge there was a Charity School in 1740 – *A Digest of Schools and Charities for Education* 1842 gives the date of the School's foundation as by Deed of 1740 but it has so far proved impossible to find the whereabouts of the School between 1740 and 1780.

A Charity Commissioners Report (1815-39) records bequests made for educating the poor children of Tonbridge:

1719	John Willard victualler	Property in Pembury and Tonbridge	£6 p.a. to put 8 boys to school for up to 3 years.
1739	Tonbridge Turnpike Trust	Interest on £100 surplus subscriptions	£5 p.a.
1740	George Putland	Rent charge from certain premises	£2.12.0d

| 1750 | Sir Thomas Hart-Dyke, Lullingstone | Property at Wrotham Shoreham and Kemsing | £9 p.a. – equal numbers of boys and girls, 2 from Eynsford, remainder from Tonbridge to inc. 2 from Hilden if eligible. |
| 1813 | John Hooker | £300 3%s | At time of Commissioners' Report this had not been received. |

There was also some funded property to the amount of £312 4s 6d, three-per-cents reduced, made up partly from balances laid out, viz. £100 in 1751 and £100 in 1808, and partly from a bequest left by a Mr Colegate.

About 1780 premises know as 'Five Elms' (referred to as Waterloo Villa in a Tonbridge Charities Report) were reputed to have been erected in what was then the Old Wells Road, now known as Waterloo Road. This building housed the Charity School, and became the National School in 1818. The Master's salary until Lady Day 1817 was £16 16s 0d, after which he was to receive £21 per annum. In 1816 the number of boys in the school was increased from 12 to 16 in prospect of the increase of income from Mr Hooker's bequest. Each boy received a suit of clothes consisting of trousers, jacket and hat – cost about one guinea – on entering the school, and no more during the time he remained there. Charity School rules stipulated that children must be clean and tidy. In a book *The Charity School Movement* by M G Jones, Dr Isaac Watts is quoted as saying that 'the clothes bestowed on Charity School children should be of the coarsest kind and the plainest form so as to distinguish them from children of better rank, as they ought to be so distinguished'.

The original ownership of 'Five Elms' is unknown. Amongst receipts in 1818 a letter from Thomas Crawtor, London, (possibly a solicitor) to the National School, refers to an interview with a William Wingfield stating 'He has required me to inform you that after taking into consideration the rent and other circumstances relative to his estate he will have no objection to allow one moiety of the expense that may be incurred relating to the sinking of a well'. There is also a receipt dated January 1820 for £40 'rent for one year' received of the Committee of the National School for William Wingfield, which suggests that the building was rented from Mr Wingfield. In 1906 the title of the property had to be accepted as commencing from the Will of the Revd Sir Charles Hardinge dated 1844; in 1840 the school-house, garden and playground was owned by Sir Charles and occupied by the Trustees of the School but the date of transfer from Mr Wingfield to Sir Charles is unknown. B Wadmore in *Some Details in the History of the Parish of Tonbridge* mentions Waterloo Villa being later converted to semi-detached villas, remaining externally the same, at a cost of £850. A picture of the house is in Frank Chapman's *Yesterday's Town*.

In 1818, when the Trustees of the Charity School (Revd Sir Charles Hardinge, John G Children, William F Woodgate and William Scoones Jnr) and the Subscribers resolved that the Charity School should become the National School, they decided that it should be conducted according to a system introduced in 1811 by Dr Andrew Bell – the Monitorial System.

In 1819 the Revd Thomas Knox, Headmaster of Tonbridge School, was Secretary to the Committee for superintending the National School. In April of that year he advertised in the Maidstone Journal for a Master. Until April 1819 Mr and Mrs Corke were in charge of the School – the date of their appointment is not known – but on 19 April 1819 a sum of £57 15s 0d was paid to Mrs Hannah Corke, being a half-year's salary of £31 10s 0d for Mr Corke (deceased) for teaching the boys, and £26 5s 0d half-year's salary to Mrs Corke for teaching the girls. In the ensuing few months various expenses were granted to a Mr David Radford on account of journeys to London, one of which was for his support during a fortnight at the Central School where he was trained in Dr Andrew Bell's Monitorial System. Mrs Corke had made two visits to the Central School, one of three weeks and one of six weeks duration. Another account – undated but obviously before Mr Corke's decease – was for maintenance by Mr Corke of two boys, 'teachers' of the National School, Seal, one for a fortnight, the other three weeks at 7s 0d each per week in order to teach them the system. The Monitorial System involved fitting the school with desks and forms to a prescribed plan; this cost the School £43 10s 0d in 1818.

The Monitorial System was, basically, the employment of a Master (or Mistress) who taught monitors only (children aged between 13 and 17). The monitors passed on the instruction to their school-fellows. The defects of the system are obvious but there were few qualified teachers at the beginning of the nineteenth century. In 1839 the Monitorial System developed into the apprenticeship of boys and girls of at least 13 years of age, and of good character, as Pupil Teachers. Monitors were paid from one to three shillings per week, according to their ability. Pupil Teachers were paid a small stipend of from £10 to £15 and the Master or Mistress given an additional £5 for training them. Pupil Teachers who were successful in passing an examination could go to a Training College. There is no record of when the National School adopted pupil teachers – nationally the scheme was adopted in 1846.

Until 1833 there is no evidence of the number of children attending the National School, but a list of Subscribers attached to the accounts for 1818-19 shows that the school had an annual income from various gentlemen of the town. When the School changed from Charity to National status some of these subscriptions were reduced from two guineas to one, or from one to half a guinea, and five gentlemen declined to subscribe.

The 1831 census gives the population of Tonbridge parish as 10,380, the parish including most of Tunbridge Wells, and Southborough and Hildenborough. Apart from private schools there were a number of schools at Tunbridge Wells and Southborough, yet in 1833 Tunbridge Wells with three schools (one each for boys, girls and infants) had 700 children who were without the means of educa-tion. In 1841 the population was Tunbridge Wells 8,000, Tonbridge Town 3,115. About one-third were under the age of sixteen. In Tonbridge approximately 180 children attended the National School; in 1847, two years after the Infant School started, 250 children attended and 75 went to a school run by the Methodists behind their chapel in Swan Lane (now East Street).

The Wesleyan Chapel was built in 1829 and had a small room at the back which was used as a Sunday School. Frederick West who was living at Tonbridge Castle (a young member of the local gentry) volunteered to help the Methodists and, finding that many of the boys who came to Sunday School did not know the alphabet, he persuaded some of them to meet him in the back room on weekdays when he instructed them in the three R's. This led to the establishment of a regular Day School which West agreed to conduct until a paid teacher could be engaged.[5] Joseph Gwynne was the first trained master but the date of his appointment can only be given as around 1850.

Tonbridge had its quota of private day and boarding schools. Clergy frequently took boys as boarders, probably teaching them English, Latin and Accounts; they would not have been poor children but had possibly been taught at home by their parents or a tutor. Generally eighteenth-century girls' boarding schools taught little of use – mostly fashionable manners![6] Teachers had no training; visiting masters were brought in, the 'Governess' or headmistress being responsible for manners. There were some good schools where conscientious women taught (or found masters to teach) languages, geography, music and singing.

Middle class children were frequently educated by their fathers, especially in the homes of clergy or grammar school teachers. Girls were taught by their mothers, if they had been educated, or along with their brothers. A few had private tutors and some were taught by male relatives who were clergymen or teachers. Upper class girls were sometimes sent to big houses to be educated and taught how to run a household – there would be the advantage of other Masters, usually language teachers.[7]

Some interesting information has been found regarding private schools in Tonbridge parish. The first known information is in Tonbridge Vestry Minutes. On 25 June 1741 it was recorded that Mrs Sarah Mercer's Boarding School for Young Gentlewomen wanted to take a pew in the gallery on the north side of the Parish Church for their use. On 2nd August it was stated that a pew was to be erected on the right hand side of the middle aisle at the entrance to the church between it and the south door. On 6 June 1763 seating then used by Mrs Chapman, mistress of a Boarding School for Young Ladies, and her pupils was appropriated for the use of Nicholas Weller of Hilden; the school were to sit in seats formerly occupied by Mrs Mercer and her pupils. Mrs Mercer was rated for her house in town between 1741 and 1753; in 1754 the house was referred to as the 'late Mrs. Mercer's'. Mrs Sarah Chapman was rated for a house near 'Houselandstyle' between 1759 and 1767 but it is not known where Mrs Mercer lived.[8]

In the Maidstone Journal of 7 September 1790 it was announced that the Revd Mr Jefferson AB proposed to open on 4th October an Academy at Tunbridge for the instruction of young Gentlemen in all the branches of useful and erudite literature including the English Grammar and the propriety of Style and Diction, which would be taught in the best and most improved method. The advertisement also stressed the importance of health and morals. The following advertisement in the Maidstone Journal for 27 December 1814 suggests it was a successful school:

> Tonbridge Academy. Rev. T. Jefferson, AB, wishing in his plan of Education to combine the Comfort and Attentions of private Tuition with the Spirit and Advantages of Public Emulation, admits only the limited number of 20 boarders.
>
> Truly grateful for past Favours, he assures his Friends and the Public that his best exertions shall never be wanting to merit the continuance of their confidence and support.
>
> The Terms, which are moderate, and the Extras very few, will be explained on application, by letter, post paid.
>
> The Academy will be opened again 23rd January 1815.

It is not known where this school was or when it was closed.

On 16 January 1810 in the Maidstone Journal Mrs and Miss Sydall informed the public that they had taken over Mrs Hankins' Ladies Boarding School at Elmden House, Tunbridge Town. Thomas Hankins, attorney, was quoted as a ratepayer between 1780 and

1803. His widow was then given as the ratepayer.[9] Presumably she started the school on the death of her husband. To quote from the advertisement:

> Miss Sydall instructs in English and French grammatically, Geography, the use of Globes, and will superintend and assist the progress of her pupils in Music, Drawing and Writing in the absence of the Masters.

The teaching of music, drawing and writing in a small private school would probably not require the services of full-time teachers so the 'absence' of the masters was possibly occasioned by their employment elsewhere; it is known that Tonbridge School employed part-time masters, certainly from around 1830, and in the 1760s a Writing Master from the town attended Tonbridge School daily after classical hours. Writing Masters usually taught writing, arithmetic and Merchants' Accounts; they often took in a few boarders (seldom more than six boys) and supplemented their incomes by giving private lessons in the homes of wealthy merchants or professional men.

Mrs and Miss Sydall were still running the school in 1813 but in 1821 it had been taken over by George Johnson and assistants. Young gentlemen were boarded and instructed in English Language, writing, arithmetic, merchants' accounts and geography at 24 guineas per annum. Greek, latin, French, Euclid's elements, plane and spherical trigonometry, algebra, astronomy, use of globes and navigation included, at 30 guineas per annum; drawing, music, dancing, on usual terms.

In 1824 Elmden House appeared in the Local Directories as a Day School for boys run by George Johnson.

W Finch's *Directory of Kent* for 1803 advertises a Writing Master, R Bass, while local directories between 1824 and 1860 advertise the following private schools, though nothing further is known of them:[10]

1826	Mrs Dillan	Preparatory School for Boys
1832-4	Edward Featherstone	Day School for Boys
1839-40	Miss Brissenden	Boarding and Day School Dry Hill House for Girls

1839-45	Henry Harris High Street	Day School for Boys
	Hannah Featherstone High Street	Day School for Girls
1839-40	Sarah Kipping Church Lane	Boarding and Day School for Girls
	Elizabeth Day High Street	Day School (unclassified)
1839-47	Misses Richardson High Street	Boarding and Day School for Girls
1839-60	Fanny Mercer High Street	Boarding and Day School for Girls

There are no records of 'dame' schools as such. From 1824 a number of schools existed for short periods, in the poorer areas of Tonbridge, which could possibly have been classified as dame schools, though the only evidence to support such a supposition is their apparent failure, and the fact that only one appears to have been started after 1859 when there were two National Schools and one Non-Conformist school in the town.

There were doubtless some small private schools, run by older women (as the title 'dame' implies) which could be classified as dame schools; they probably taught the alphabet, elementary reading and counting, and charged only a few pence per week to supplement a small private income. They possibly fulfilled a much-felt need before National Schools were started. However, nationally they were frequently run by women who were unfit for any other employment; many were carried on by so-called teachers who were engaged at the same time in other employment – shop-keeping, sewing, laundry etc. They were often housed in dilapidated garrets or damp cellars, especially in the larger towns. Some, regrettably, owed their existence to the mistress's desire for gin! All charged a fee of a few pence per week. There were schools for older children, taught by schoolmasters, a few of which were well-run, but in many cases the masters were from the very dregs of society.[11]

Before the advent of charity schools teachers of the poor had no professional status and were often not only illiterate but morally unfit to teach children. When the Society for Promoting Christian Knowledge took over the organisation of charity schools in 1698 they drafted the qualifications which they considered necessary. A master should be a Communicant of the Church of England, not under the age of 25 years, be of sober life and conversation, of meek temper and humble behaviour, have a good government of himself and his passions, and have a good genius for teaching. The same religious and practical qualifications were demanded for women teachers, except that few were required to teach writing, and fewer still arithmetic.

In the early eighteenth century there were few books suitable for children – they were taught to read from the Book of Common Prayer. The Bible and Aesop's Fables provided the literature approved by Charity Schools, with *The Whole Duty of Man* given as a school-leaving present. Boys who could read and write were taught arithmetic. Girls were taught plain needle-work, knitting and sometimes spinning.

The average salary of a master in a London school at the beginning of the eighteenth century was £30 a year with coals and sometimes a house rent free. For a woman £24 was the maximum, usually less. In the country £20 was offered. Tonbridge records reveal an interesting comparison between the salary paid to the Master of Holmes School in Southborough in 1785, £42, and that paid to the Master of the Tonbridge Charity School up to 1817, which was £16 16s 0d, later raised to £21!

There are few records of the Charity School but a study of schools in the early nineteenth century is some indication of conditions in the eighteenth century.[11] In the nineteenth century Log Books had to be kept by teachers for each school; these paint a poignant picture of school life which is not available for the charity school. Records from Bank Street School in the 1850s suggest great poverty in the town.

At the beginning of the nineteenth century Dr A Bell had developed a system of education, however inadequate, but in 1805 this gentleman had said, 'It is not proposed that the children of the poor be educated in an expensive manner, or even taught to write and cypher. There is a risk of elevation, by an indescriminate education, of the minds of those doomed to the drudgery of daily labour above their condition, thereby rendering them discontented and unhappy in their lot'. By the middle of the nineteenth century Tonbridge Churches were making good progress towards providing somewhat better education for all poor children in the town.

References

1   Hans, N, *New Trends in Education in the Eighteenth Century*
2   Speck, W H, *Stability and Strife*
3   Pinchbeck, I and Hewitt, M, *Children in English Society*
4   Benge Burr, T, *History of Tunbridge Wells*
5   Neve, A H, *The Tonbridge of Yesterday* (Tonbridge, 1933)
6   Gardener, D, *English Girlhood at School*
7   Pinchbeck, I and Hewitt, M, *Children in English Society*
8   *Overseers Accounts,* Centre for Kentish Studies P371/12/4,5
9   *Overseers Accounts,* Centre for Kentish Studies P371/12/4,5
10   Bagshaw, S, and Pigot's *Directories*
11   Curtis, S J, *History of Education in Great Britain*

Tonbridge School
1714–1840

Sally Hedley-Jones

Tonbridge School in the eighteenth century was not the major public school of more recent times, but a country market town grammar school. It was in the better class of grammar schools, not a 'great' one, such as Eton, but a 'gentleman's' school nonetheless – a distinction made by R S Thompson in his study of eighteenth century grammar schools.[1] Previous accounts of the school in this period have relied heavily on tradition and the School Lists (the annual register of pupils). These Lists are a valuable primary source, but because they are an incomplete series they must be used in conjunction with other sources, such as the Governors' Minutes at Skinners' Hall. However, the records for any eighteenth century school are sparse to say the least, and accounts of individual institutions depend a great deal on comparisons with others, and can only be conjectural.

That Tonbridge was not an insignificant school in this period is due, in part, to the area and the town in which it was situated. It was well placed educationally within the county with only Sevenoaks grammar school in the immediate locality with which to share the local gentry pupils. The other grammar schools in the county tended to be in the east – such as Maidstone or Canterbury. Compared with the rest of the country at this time, Kent did not have as many schools as Yorkshire (about 58) but with around 20 it had more than its neighbours of Sussex (10), and Essex (15). There were enough gentry families in the Tonbridge vicinity to keep the grammar school and its reputation maintained, and to make sure that the rights of the Foundationers (local boys; the name was not used until 1825) were observed. The latter were also watched carefully by the town as a whole, although their concern (particularly towards the end of the century when educational needs were changing) lay more in safeguarding the charity left by Sir Andrew Judde and Sir Thomas Smythe than with educational interests.

Geographically the town was ideally placed – a major centre for communications and transport within the county, and equidistant between London and the coastal resorts. 'The experience of nearly three hundred years has proved that the situation [of the school] is remarkably salubrious', wrote J Clifton in his 1837 *Tunbridge Wells Guide*. Twenty seven years previously G A Cooke in *A Description of the County of Kent* remarked on '... the principal street ... which is broad and airy ... naturally neat and clean, and constantly kept in that state under the care of two wardens'. On his arrival as Headmaster in 1843 Dr Welldon boasted that 'I am bound to say we had very little ill-health in the School'. This despite the open drain which ran down Bordyke and 'often smells very offensively' (Revd E H Welldon).

The school's success was also due in equal part to the educational reputation it had built up over the centuries. 'It has always maintained a good reputation, as well for the learning of the scholars educated at it, as the eminent abilities of the Masters who have had from time to time the care of it', wrote E Hasted in 1798.[2] The school seems to have regularly attracted Masters who were notables already in their own right, not necessarily in the field of education. The fact that the Governors were an important City Livery Company may have appealed to a better type of schoolmaster. The Governors 'deserve particular commendation, as a retrospection for many years past will show that their choice [of Master] has generally fallen on men of very distinguished and eminent abilities'.[3] They even gave Richard Spencer (Master 1714-43) an annuity after his retirement because he had 'not been able to lay up a sufficiency to support him in his old age', according to the Court Book report for April 1743. Furthermore a Master at Tonbridge was entitled to the generous allowance of a 'dwelling rent free' and a regular salary from the Governors regardless of fluctuations in pupil numbers.

What the eighteenth century Grammar School looked like can only be guessed at by looking at several contemporary prints and surviving photographs of it, and a model in the school library. The

Tonbridge School as it was from 1760 to 1825, from W G Hart's *Register of Tonbridge School 1553-1820* (Source: Tonbridge School Library)

main building resembled the traditional image of a grammar school with its central schoolroom, dormitories under the eaves and a bell turret on the roof. At the southern and northern ends were the Master's and Usher's dwellings respectively. The school building was set back from the High Street and ran from the south side of the 1859 chapel to the south end of the present Headmaster's house. At various times alterations were made to the structure, notably around 1760 when James Cawthorn added to the south end what is now known as Skinners' Library, and in 1826 when a new dining and dormitory block were built behind the Master's house. There was a gravel play yard behind the main building, gardens for the Master and Usher, and several outbuildings including an infirmary and brewhouse. More information on the site and its surroundings can be pieced together from references in the Governors' Minutes. The 'well-built venerable structure' was demolished in 1863 – only the 1760 and 1826 additions are extant today, although many of the old stones were used for the stable block in Lansdowne Road.[4]

Until the nineteenth century the area covered by the school remained much the same as at its foundation in the sixteenth century. In 1823, in anticipation of expansion following the implementation of the New Scheme, the Governors looked for more land in the vicinity of the school. They disregarded the Ferox estate because 'no part of the Residence or other erections on the estate could be converted to any ... efficient purpose'.[5] Instead, they bought the property of Thomas Martin which included what is now the Upper and Lower Hundreds and the Head – then hop and pasture land – and the house now known as Old Judde. The extent of this land was marked by iron boundary posts which are still visible in The Avenue and in front of the Science Building.

The most tangible impact that the school had on the town should be reflected in the number of local boys (Foundationers) who went there. However, only a rough idea of who attended and between exactly which years is possible because the School Lists are incomplete and often only give the surnames taken at each Visitation. Foundationers are rarely specifically denoted in these lists, and although it is possible to identify some local names, (such as Woodgate, Mills, Scoones or Hooker), these belong mainly to the well known gentry or professional families and may not be truly representative of local boys' attendance. It should be remembered that the school was intended under Sir Andrew Judde's charter to be open to all local boys who could read and write some English and Latin and pay sixpence a year to the book fund – irrespective of social background.

However, a rough estimation of the ratio of day boys to boarders over the period can be drawn up. It reveals that Thomas Knox's statement to the 1819 Charity Commission that 'six [Foundationers] has been above the average for the last 4-score years' out of an average class of 50 pupils was largely true:

Year	size of class	no. of day boys	
1764	62	9	
1770	44	3	
1775	22	9	
1788	63	16	(but 5 Burling brothers were there at the same time)

1794	26	7
1811	39	7
1819	42	10

From the beginning of the period covered, the School Lists describe all pupils as 'The Young Gentlemen'. Even taking into account the fact that the background of some boys is unidentifiable, the majority of pupils had fathers who were gentlemen – clergymen, doctors, lawyers or of no profession. By the end of the eighteenth century the range of occupations did widen considerably to include some of the new middle classes: civil servants, army officers and London merchants. Occasionally an aristocratic pupil can be found, such as the son of Sir Charles Whitworth, baronet of Leybourne Grange, in 1761-65, and the heir of the 7th Baron Kircudbright in 1782, or one whose father held an important Government post – Sampson Gideon, financier to Lord Pitt, or William Suckling, Commissioner in the Customs Office. But the majority were gentlemen.

Nonetheless, there are names in the Lists which are identifiable as local, but who were not from the gentry classes. For example, Humphrey Steer (1763-64), son of the man 'att ye Crowne', John Slatter (1775-84), William Brissenden (1759-62), J Tworte (1781) or George Wise (1825-31). And the list of constables and borsholders for the Manor of Tonbridge (1740-56) shows that the majority of those holding the office were either fathers of pupils or old boys themselves. These men could be classed as better-off tradesmen and craftsmen, but some, including boys not identifiable in the Lists, may have been from the poorer classes.

However, such an indication, that the local attendance in the eighteenth century was drawn mainly from the gentry and professional classes may not be as misrepresentative as it seems: 'As prices rose, a full course grammar school and university education became a more and more remote possibility for the poorer classes'.[6] This too was Thomas Knox's assumption, in the 1819 Charity Commission Report: 'the reason of the small number of Foundation scholars ... is probably the little importance attached by the inhabitants of Tonbridge to an education simply classical for their sons'. They preferred a more practical education, if one was wanted at all, and the subsequent period at university was probably financially unviable anyway. A letter by the Revd Johnson Towers from the 1760s shows that at Tonbridge Foundationers were able to learn the other subjects offered to boarders provided they paid for them: French £2 2s a year, writing and accounts £1 4s 9d, dancing £2 15s. It was a trend found throughout the whole grammar school system, and is reflected in the number of alternative educational establishments springing up in this period, (Towers' letter goes on to mention that 'boys in general who are intended for trade go from me to some academy about 13 or 14 years of age'.)

Although boys did come from beyond the parish and county boundaries, increasingly so over the period, Tonbridge at this time never completely lost its local pupils, because it maintained the Foundationers' charity and was the type of town to always have a 'small, but stable core of professional men'.[7] They were the class who bettered themselves socially through education by taking advantage of those Foundation rights. How many parents moved to the area specifically for this purpose is not known, but it can be speculated that a fair number did so; possibly they included the Woodgates and Childrens who both arrived at the beginning of the eighteenth century. As late as 1827 Mrs Acton moved from Ipswich to the town, sent her son Edgar to the school and took boarders in her Bordyke house. (Her daughter, Eliza, created 'The Monitors Tart' or 'Tourte à la Judd' and 'Bordyke Bread'.) The Lade family from Sussex sent their sons to the school in order that they might better themselves and thus inherit their great-uncle's fortune.[8] The Austens are also a good example – a central Kent cloth industry family who moved near to the grammar schools at Sevenoaks and Tonbridge, and became local professionals (apothecary and surgeon), and in the next generation were university educated, gentlemen clergymen and married well.

It was the local gentry boys who were most likely to have had fathers at the school: it was even more common to find their cousins there. For example, George Austen (1741-47), and his first cousin Henry Austen, were contemporaries at the school, as were George's half-brother William Hampson Walter of Parsonage Farm, and Henry's three future Hooker brothers-in-law. William Scoones, solicitor, was an Old Tonbridgian (1755-62), as were his father Thomas, his three sons and four grandsons. George Children went to the school (1750-58), as did his father, two uncles, two nephews, his niece's husband, his own son, and his daughter-in-law's brother.

The boys who came to the Grammar School under Thomas Knox at the beginning of the nineteenth century still show a sizeable local attendance, but there is a definite change in the makeup of names. There are fewer of the eighteenth century traditional ones of Woodgate and Children, and more the names that characterise the nineteenth century history of the school and the town – Wadmore, Carnell, Goldsmid, Gorham, Beeching and Cox.

Fee-paying non-Foundation boarders became increasingly more important to the school over the century and W G Hart's estimation that the majority of pupils were this type seems correct from reading the Lists.[9] Again, this was a trend reflected in all grammar schools as the original value of foundations decreased. In the school itself no physical distinction was made between Foundationers and non-Foundationers. 'Either in or out of school hours ... I encourage them to mix together', wrote Thomas Knox in 1819. However this had not always been the state of affairs. In 1763 the town, 'in Public Vestry assembled', complained to the Governors that 'the present Master has lately in more than one instance insisted that it [permission] should be asked of him as a favour before admission, which the inhabitants apprehend is a manifest injustice and contrary to the will of the founder'.[10] The Governors repeatedly delayed making a decision, so the town under its solicitor, William Scoones, sought the opinion of several notable lawyers. Their opinion supported the town's view and the Governors conceded. It was also legally decided that the Foundation rights applied to the whole parish of Tonbridge and not just the town. Lest it be forgotten, the judgement was published on a board in the Parish Church porch. It was an event indicative of how seriously the town took its charitable entitlement from Sir Andrew Judde, and also how much they wanted to maintain good relations with their benefactors – insisting that they wished to avoid litigation, and excusing the Governors' opinions as 'hastily formed or founded on some misapprehension'.[11] However, they can have placated the school little by taking the opportunity at the same time to assess the Poor Rate paid by the school, and deciding that the amount should be forty shillings a year.

Considering the developments in other grammar schools at this time, the Foundationers at Tonbridge did not fare badly. Their charity was maintained even after 1825 when classical tuition still remained free to them and they were given preferential treatment in the awarding of Exhibitions; and until quite recently day boys were allowed ten pounds off their fees.

The town benefited not only from sending its sons free of charge to the school, but its economy also gained from the supplies of food, servants, clothes and other everyday provisions. Townspeople also took in boarding pupils – Sir Andrew Judde had clearly intended this when in the Statutes he restricted the Master's quota of boarders to twelve, and ordered that it was his duty to check the suitability of the town houses taking in boys: 'the party that taketh the scholar ... to board shall faithfully promise to the Master ... to keep them continually from all unthrifty pastimes and gaming in his house'. Unfortunately there are no accounts of life as a boarder in a town house, although several survive from those in Thomas Knox's house, and it is clear from these that the board and lodging paid for was very basic, pupils having to supply their own cutlery, cooking utensils and some food. Nor is much known about who in the town took in boarders. In Pigot's Directory for 1832-34, Mrs Williams in the High Street, Mrs Elizabeth Acton in Bordyke, and the Revd Glover Mungeam were listed as boarding house owners specifically 'for the young gentlemen attending the Grammar School'.

The 1825-26 New Scheme for the school was the result of an extra four thousand pounds a year generated from building work by James Burton and other builders on the Saint Pancras lands of Sir Andrew Judde at the beginning of the nineteenth century (See p. 73). However, the Skinners' Company argued that such money belonged to them and was surplus to the financial needs of the Grammar School. The town took up the argument of Thomas Knox, then Master, that Judde's will intended all the money from these lands to go to the charity it represented. In 1819 a bill was filed in Chancery to resolve the dispute and the Governors faced the town's representatives who were the vicar Sir Charles Hardinge, churchwarden John Harmer, John Luxford of Ferox Hall, and James Eldridge West, all under the leadership of William Scoones. Judgement was given in favour of the school and town in 1820, and a new scheme for the use of the money was drawn up. The town had hoped and suggested that the money might be used to provide a new commercial school for their use – but they had to wait another sixty years for the Company to fulfil that wish.

Mention has already been made of the contribution by boarders to the town's economy, but the School also helped it in other ways too. From the Governors' Minutes it appears that all the Masters of the school were concerned about its physical upkeep, and they constantly submitted estimates for repairs deemed necessary. The annual cost of repairs (where known) for the previous twenty years was given in the 1819 Charity Commissioners Report:

1797	£36	1803	£108	1808	£520	1814	£596
1799	£180	1804	£264	1809	£112	1815	£135
1800	£32	1805	£200	1811	£163	1816	£251
1801	£40	1806	£400	1812	£122	1817	£124
1802	£113	1807	£294	1813	£105	1818	£107

To carry out these repairs they employed a variety of workmen and craftsmen, and by the mid-eighteenth century there was clearly an established works staff. Moreover, the same names (individuals and families) recur in the reports of repairs over the period. Not only were they responsible for major structural alterations such as 'pulling down the chimney in the brewhouse and rebuilding the same',[12] but they also carried out everyday repairs like 'such plastering and white washing and painting as shall be necessary ... in the school room'.[13]

The repair bills were carefully scrutinised by the Governors for expensive work. Mary Ball (painter) was asked to submit an itemised bill in 1759 on suspicion of having charged for unnecessary work, 'specifying the particular places where the work charged therein was done and also what price she charges per yard for the painting work'. She was replaced soon afterwards as painter to the school by John Feldwick.

In 1743 only a carpenter, James Norris, appears in the records, but by 1747 there were also Jacob Mercer (bricklayer), William Crundall (glazier) and Gilbert Dryland (smith). Gradually the staff built up – in 1753 Harry Ball (painter and pumpmaker) first appears, by 1770 Henry Sidney (founder), and in 1793 William Feldwick (paperhanger). Others included John Town (mason, 1762), E Baker (paperhanger, 1765), Robert Burgess (smith, 1773), Thomas King (carpenter, 1779), and Richard Luck (smith, 1786). Family concerns included the Wellers, paperhangers (James, 1773 and John, 1780), the Mercers, bricklayers (Jacob, 1747 and Thomas, 1769), the Feldwicks, paperhangers (already mentioned), and William Brissenden, carpenter in 1755, whose concern was taken over by Sarah Brissenden (presumably his wife) in 1770. Harry Ball's name as painter was replaced by that of the aforementioned Mary Ball in 1757, again presumably his wife.

The majority of these workmen were local – they (or their relatives) appear in Directories from the end of the eighteenth century, in the 1748 Churchwardens' Accounts of Parish Ratepayers, and in the lists of Manor Court Officers (constables and borsholders). It is also known that James Norris was a Town Warden. Robert Mercer, bricklayer and presumably of the same family who did work for the school, and William Feldwick, school paperhanger, also did work for Samuel Mills, gentleman of Tonbridge, according to his executors' accounts. In 1792 Feldwick proposed buying the house he rented off Mills, and by 1829-30 according to Pigot's Directory he was classed as a 'gentleman'. Perhaps these school workmen were leading craftsmen in the town who worked on other important civic amenities such as the Parish Church.

George Luck, pupil at the Grammar School in 1775, was possibly the son of Richard Luck, smith to the school, and it is known that

William and Sarah Brissenden sent their son William (1759-62); but there is no firm evidence to suggest other workmen did likewise. Certainly similar surnames do appear in the Lists over the century, and therefore it is quite possible these pupils were the men themselves, their sons or their relatives.

The town probably also provided the domestic household of the school. The details of the servants in the Master's and Usher's houses in 1841 under Thomas Knox are known from the Census. Knox had six female servants, aged between 53 and 20, and two male servants, aged 60 and 20; his usher had three female servants, aged 20, 25 and 35, and one male servant aged 15. It is likely that previous Masters had similarly sized establishments; but it is not known whether any of these servants worked also for the school in its laundry, kitchen, dairy, bakehouse or brewhouse, or whether they were exclusively part of the Master's household.

As well as an impact on the economic life of the town, there was also some social interaction between the two, although that involving the gentry is better documented than that for the less well-off inhabitants. In an issue of *The Tonbridgian* in 1858 one boy wrote 'We know that Tonbridge is what most people would call a dull place and depends in a great measure on the school for having its dullness periodically dispelled'. According to J F Wadmore's memoirs,[14] there was an annual cricket match between the town and the school, (perhaps there were other sporting encounters too). '... Waite, who always played in top boots, was one of the stoutest and steadiest, if not the most agile, batsman on the side of the town, who used to muster in strong force as spectators ... sitting in groups on the slopes, smoking their pipes and drinking the barrels of beer and cider which were placed under the trees that line the south side of the ground'.

Less harmonious were the encounters between the school boys and town boys. Albany de Fonblanque (1842-46) has left a vivid description of such a meeting: 'There was a frontier tribe in a row of cottages on the London Road to the right of the gate at the end of The Avenue ... they constantly attacked us – or we them. A sort of

"Town and Gown" row was chronic ... we called out the fencing-class with their basket handled single-sticks, and there was lamentation and woe'. An alternative reaction was recalled in an 1865 article in *The Tonbridgian:* 'It was not unusual for both sides to be seized with a panic at precisely the same moment and to gallop away frantically in opposite directions'.

The annual Visitation by the Governors provided the opportunity for the ordinary townspeople to see the descendants of their sixteenth and seventeenth century charitable benefactors, 'of whom they have heard so much since their infancy' wrote Dr Knox in 1799.[15] For the gentry it was a day of immense social activity, certainly by the eighteenth century. Originally, the Visitation was meant only for the purpose of seeing and considering 'whether the School Master and Usher do their duties towards their scholars in teaching them virtue and learning; and whether the scholars do of their part use themselves virtuous and studious'. The proceedings of a typical Visitation day in the eighteenth century have been described by Gilbert Hoole in his *Tonbridge Miscellany,* based on a Court Book report of 1791.[16] The Governors stayed at the Rose and Crown (known as the Crown until 1787), and dined there when the proceedings at the school were finished. The 'whole company, which consists, besides the visitors and their friends, of the neighbouring gentry and the clergy',[17] were invited to the dinner, the Examination, and the evening entertainment provided by the Master. It is no surprise therefore that the event did become one of 'very considerable expense' for the Skinners, and in 1782 and 1795 they gave an order to the Master to cut down on the numbers by issuing formal invitations for dinner.

Yet the Skinners did not forget the ordinary townspeople on their Visitation, and paid for a dinner of 'three fowls, bacon and greens or fillet of veal, and a plumb [sic] pudding' with a bottle of wine each for the churchwardens and 'others of the parish'.[18] The Governors also processed to a service in the Parish Church 'where they distribute bread, money, and cloaths to a number of poor persons of the parishes of Tunbridge, Bidborough and Speldhurst according to the will of Sir Thomas Smith'.[19] There was a note in 1745 that the cloth had been delayed because the ship from Hull could not sail without a convoy. During Thomas Knox's mastership the towns-people were also involved in the preparation for the festivities, helping the boys who spent the day before the Examination gathering flowers with which to decorate the school. They traditionally gave the boys 'refreshment' as well, until one boy was found to be 'unfit' for examination on his return, and the practice was stopped in 1833.

The links of individual Masters with the town are not well documented prior to the Knoxes' mastership, if indeed there were any. It is probable that as clergymen they helped at services in the Parish Church. James Cawthorn and all three Knox Masters were buried in the Parish Church, as were some of their relatives, and those of Richard Spencer. All who had sons sent them to the school (except for Doctor Vicesimus Knox who was sent to Merchant Taylors). Thomas Knox was an Old Tonbridgian Master, but not the first.

It is believed that the Revd James Cawthorn, (Master 1743-61) wrote the elegy on Richard Children's monument in the Parish Church. A witness to his own will was Thomas Austen, whose son Henry left the school in the year after the Master's arrival, and whose nephew, George, was one of Cawthorn's ushers. Cawthorn is also mentioned in the 1748 Churchwardens Accounts of Parish Ratepayers for 'part of the King's Head'. However, despite these hints of familiarity with the local community, there is no solid evidence for interaction between Cawthorn and the townspeople, social or otherwise. According to his will he was buried in the Parish Church beneath the school's north aisle gallery, the 'expenses to be no more than commonly decent'.

Virtually the same situation applies to his successor, the Revd Johnson Towers, for whom it is known that he had as witnesses to his own will William Turner, William Scoones and Thomas Miller; slightly more revealing though in Towers' case is the reference to the executor of the will – George Children as 'my worthy friend', also making him guardian of Towers' son. Children was bequeathed ten guineas by the will to 'buy him a ring to wear in remembrance of me', and in 1819 his son, John George Children, married the widow of Towers junior as his third wife.

All that is known of the Revd Vicesimus Knox is that he had William and Thomas Scoones as witnesses to his will and that he retired to Penshurst from the school in 1778. However, it is with the Revd Vicesimus' son, Dr Vicesimus Knox, that there is clear evidence of a close relationship between the Master and local gentry; and with his son, Dr Thomas Knox, with the town also. When the latter died, he was mourned in the '... town and neighbourhood ... [for] the awfully sudden death of their respected minister and fellow towns-man' (George Wise).

The 'elegant Doctor Knox' was a noted educationalist, essayist and preacher throughout the whole country. The Woodgate letters reveal just how much local socialising he did as well, with frequent entertainments and receptions at the school House. The oft quoted remark by Henry Woodgate in 1781 bears this out: 'Mr Knox has a new coach just come out spick & span with a pair of long Tail Greys. Is this not quite the thing. My Aunt says "Lor, Sir, a schoolmasters is a vast fine trade"'.[20] It was under Knox that the evening entertain-ments on Visitation Day appear to begin. In 1795, in the evening, the ladies 'were entertained for nearly two hours with verses from the pen of Dr Knox ... truly deserving of the praise which they experi-enced'.[21] His wife Mary's family, the Millers, were established Tonbridge professionals and Old Tonbridgians, and were reputedly descended from Thomas Roots, Master from 1668 to 1714.

Dr Knox was familiar enough with ordinary town life to be able to recommend to the Governors the best day on which to hold their Visitation, considering the various markets held and the possible effect of such an event on the local population: 'I conjecture that as many oxen and other cattle are driven about the Town on that day the Procession in the morning to the Church may be disturbed ... that the inns will all be full'.[22] The surviving lists of Tonbridge inhabitants liable to serve on juries at the Manor Court cite Dr Knox between the years 1793 and 1806 (some years are missing). He retired in 1812 to London, although he continued as curate of

Shipbourne, and died while on a visit to his son, Thomas, now himself Master of the Grammar School.

Thomas Knox, who had grown up at the school with the local gentry boys, married one of their sisters in 1815 – Frances Woodgate of Summerhill. He continued to play a part in social gatherings as his father had done: 'I spent a pleasant evening with Mr and Mrs Knox on Tuesday; Mr and Mrs Hardinge, Miss Callendar, Sir William [West] and his nephew and a small party dined there'.[23] In 1843, on his death following a heart attack in the Church vestry, the mourning and funeral showed just how much a part he must also have played in the daily life of the town. George Wise, the Tunbridge Ware manufacturer and Old Tonbridgian, has left an account of it: all the shops closed, the coffin was followed by a crocodile procession of around 170 local tradesmen and gentlemen 'present on the solemn occasion to denote their respect for the deceased', to a Church 'crowded to excess ... we never witnessed a more imposing funeral ceremony'. An elegy was written by an anonymous townsman (now in the town library archives); John Carnell (solicitor) was witness to his will.

With the death of Thomas Knox, the eighteenth century period for both the town and the school can be said to have properly ended. For two and a half centuries the two had interacted, each able to profit from the other's existence. The eighteenth century school had played a central role in the town's life because it influenced the economy – provisions and employment – the social life at all levels, and it educated the classes which governed the town. There is no doubt that having a successful grammar school helped put the town 'on the map', not only in the county but further afield. But by 1843 the educational provision – the fundamental contact between school and town, was no longer felt necessary nor desirable by the majority of townspeople, and neither was it financially viable any more from the school's point of view.

Main sources

Governors' Minutes (Court Books), Skinners' Hall (see note below)
Hart, W G, *The Register of Tonbridge School 1553-1820*, 1935
Hoole, G P, *A Tonbridge Miscellany*, 1985

Hughes-Hughes, W O, *The Register of Tonbridge School 1826-93*, 1893
Rivington, S, *The History of Tonbridge School*, 1947
Thompson, R S, *Classics or Charity? The Dilemma of the Eighteenth Century Grammar School*, 1971
Woodgate, G and G M G, *A History of the Woodgates of Stonewall Park and of Somerhill in Kent, and their Connections* (Wisbech [1910])
Archive material in Tonbridge Public Library and the Centre for Kentish Studies, Maidstone.

The Governors' Minutes are part of the Skinners' Company Court Books – large volumes of untranscribed material kept at the Company's Hall. They began to be kept from the mid-sixteenth century and record the minutes of the meetings of the governing body of the Company held weekly. The entries relating to the school are of a very routine nature – Visitation arrangements, repairs to the fabric and the appointment of new Masters.

Notes

1 *Classics or Charity?, 1972*, pp28-29
2 *The History and Topographical Survey of the County of Kent*, volume 5, p247
3 *Gentleman's Magazine*, 1779
4 Ireland, W H, *A New and Complete History of the County of Kent*, 1829
5 Hoole, G, *A Tonbridge Miscellany*, 1985, p37
6 Thompson, R S, *Classics or Charity?*, 1972, p27
7 Chalklin, C W, *The Provincial Towns of Georgian England*, 1974, p6
8 Hart, W G, *The Old School Lists*, 1933
9 *The Register of Tonbridge School*, 1935, p14
10 *Vestry Minutes*, 1763
11 Ibid
12 *Court Book*, 1753
13 *Court Book*, 1757
14 in Rivington, S, *The History of Tonbridge School*, 1947
15 Hoole, G, *A Tonbridge Miscellany*, 1985, p68
16 Ibid pp65-67
17 Carlisle, N, *A Concise Description of the Endowed Grammar Schools*, 1818, p631
18 *Court Book*, 1783
19 Hasted, E, *The History ... [of] Kent*, p247
20 *History of the Woodgates*, 1910, p247
21 Ibid p335
22 Hoole, G, *A Tonbridge Miscellany*, 1985, pp67-68
23 *History of the Woodgates*, 1910, p205

Five properties on the Outskirts of Tonbridge, 1740–1840

Margaret Stephens

Introduction

> 'Battel, Wednesday, Aug. 3, 1752 ... We lay last night at Tonbridge Town ... The inn was full of farmers and tobacco ... we all the while up to the head and ears in a market of sheep and oxen.'
>
> Horace Walpole[1]

The first Tuesday in the month was the day of the important stock and cattle market in the High Street opposite the Rose and Crown. The Georgian visitor seeking a horse or a bed had to jostle with farmers and dealers every Friday as well for that was the day of the weekly general market.

In this document-based study the focus is on five properties of varying size on the outskirts of the Town for the century following 1740. They skirt the Town from the north to the south-east and the farthest of the five was no more than an hour's walk from the centre of the Town, that is, the Rose and Crown itself. They were selected only because there is, for each, sufficient evidence to build up a reasonably coherent picture of ownership, tenancies, and land use. The social standing of owners and some tenants will be given attention while there will be an exploration, also, of relationships between them within this community of close-knit public and private lives.

Interwoven with these socio-economic strands is the theme of the use of the land itself, which was the concern of all whether directly or indirectly. Three of the properties are agricultural, one more residential and the fifth commercial in use. Because information on the period of the French Wars and the decades following is patchy, concentration will be on the earlier decades of our period, and then on the Tithe evidence of 1838.

163

The properties in the eighteenth century

The Cage and Starvecrow

The Cage farmhouse, with its outbuildings, formed the nucleus of a discrete farm of about 400 acres, but was held in this period with part of Starvecrow and meadows beyond the Hadlow Road, towards the Medway. The whole estate will be considered as one for this study, although the units were leased out separately. The Pen Stream, flowing from the North Frith to cross the Shipbourne Road at Frog Bridge, and then continuing south-east to the Stair and out to join the many streams which form the Medway to the east of the Town, was the boundary of the parishes of Hadlow and Tonbridge, and formed a natural dividing line between Starvecrow and Cage farms. An estate map of 1767 shows the two farms and the meadows as belonging to Mr Alchin.[2]

The map shows field names and sizes. 'Marlpits' and 'Kiln Fields' indicate contemporary or past use. There is a seven-acre hop garden, and an orchard near the farmstead. The largest field is of 13 acres, and, as would be expected, the larger fields are the ones under the plough. The only meadow on the main Cage is near the Pen Stream. The name 'Denshire Field' on the site of the present Denbeigh estate, indicates the process of burning earth or 'denshiring' to produce ash as fertiliser. Nearby, abutting to the Shipbourne Road, were Upper and Lower Thistly Fields, totalling 19 acres.

North of the present Whistler Road were two fields known as Starvecrow Fields, but most of the rest of the eastern Starvecrow was woodland.

Overall the impression from these names is one of heavy soil needing careful working, and ploughing by oxen would be expected.

A lease of 1733 names three areas on the Cage which were pasture and to remain as such. These were Great and Little Pen Meads, and Stack Platt near the farmstead. They totalled 21 acres. The Cage itself was a mixed, that is a predominantly arable, farm.

Parsonage Farm

This was only a fourteen-acre site which could not have been a viable farm. The homestead was near the site of the recently demolished Yardley Court, and the land ran east to west parallel with Yardley Park Road, but it is likely that access to the Farm was mainly from the Hadlow Road. Four of the fourteen acres lay on the other side of the Shipbourne Road. As there was a small farm called the 'Nunnery' adjacent to the Parsonage and as one of the fields attached to the Parsonage was called Church Field, it may be that this area belonged originally to the Parish Church.

In 1754 there were a Forestall and Lower Slip mentioned in a deed, and these are confirmed in the Tithe as forming the driveway out to the Shipbourne Road.[3] There was also a Barn Meadow, indicating the storage of hay, but we can presume that, rather than being agricultural land, this must have been a 'suburban' residence, with perhaps a few animals, and fruit for domestic use.

Stair Farm

The Old Hadlow Road makes a dog-leg as it crosses the Pen Stream and near this point was the entrance to Stair Farm. The homestead itself stands on higher ground overlooking the broad floodplain of the Medway, with Somerhill beyond. The farmland ran down to the first watercourse feeding into the main River and curved round in a north-easterly direction towards Fish Hall. The farm, a small one of about 60 acres, was in the Parish of Hadlow in our period.

Adjacent to Stair Farm on the west was a stretch of land which, in 1748, according to an estate map, belonged to Robert Simmons.[4] This straddled the Hadlow Road and extended up to Higham Lane and just beyond it. This farm was later known as 'Winchester' and will be relevant in the later part of this study.

Leases exist for the Stair in the eighteenth century and will be analysed later, but little is known of how the farm was managed. In 1785 the owner laid down that clover was to be sown to act as manure to nourish some of the land for an incoming tenant. Fruit trees were important but it is not clear what acreage was planted as

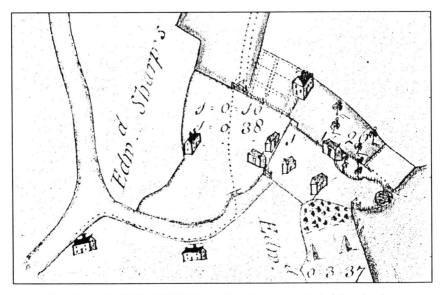

Stair Farm in 1748. Old Hadlow Road runs up the left hand side.
(Source: Centre for Kentish Studies)

orchard. What is clear is the weight given to the treatment of the soil with marl or lime. In 1754 it was covenanted that 256 bushels of either should be laid on each field. It is now thought that early use of marl and lime was excessive, and that only lime should be considered for clay soil.

Although outside Tonbridge Parish the farm is included because it was held by Tonbridge residents, and its farmers would have used the Town markets.

The Tanyard

This was a four-acre site close to the Old Mill with access to Mill Lane, and thence to the Postern or to the Hadlow Road. By tradition tanneries were situated on the periphery of towns because of the foul smell from the skins in the vats. The workshops here consisted of the 'Tan House, Cistern and Tannfatts'.[6]

No eighteenth century map has been found but a survey of Sir Thomas Fane's land in 1699 shows a rectangular parcel of land with one building besides the Mill, labelled Puxty's Land.[7] As manorial rentals refer to Twort's Tanyard as 'late Puxty's' it can be presumed that this was the site[8] although the building shown does not appear to have access to the Mill Stream and this would have been necessary for a tannery. The present Grove House does have that proximity. The tanners paid a quit rent to the Manor of 10d. By this period all the manorial rents had become insignificant.

Harry Twort senior and junior held the Tanyard over most of the century and developed gardens, an orchard and hopgarden. Their dwelling-house was called Sanguins.

North of their forestall abutting onto the Hadlow Road was, in 1699, a hopgarden named Gunnings. This and a further seven acres of meadow, was purchased by Henry Eldridge, tanner, towards the end of the eighteenth century, and he had a second house built on the site about this time. He explains these additions in his son's marriage settlement of 1809. The area was now almost square, stretching from the Hadlow Road to Swan Mead.

The Postern area

The whole area embraced about 400 acres, stretching from the Tudeley stream to the east to Postern Heath to the west, from the Medway to the north to lands abutting onto Tudeley Lane to the south.

Like the Cage, this was demesne land of the Manor of Tonbridge, but had been partitioned in the seventeenth century. While the lord of the Manor retained a parcel until the end of the eighteenth century, the rest gradually changed hands, by means which are not altogether clear. Also, some holdings seem to have expanded or contracted as fields were reapportioned. Homesteads fluctuated as they were built, rebuilt, neglected or demolished. According to Savills, the estate agents, Postern House was built in 1757. The Old Forge and Saxby's (Rat's Castle) deteriorated and were subdivided. A survey of 1674/5 shows an early Postern House to the east of the present one.[9] Postern Park was the seat of John H West who held gentry balls there from the end of the eighteenth century, so was no doubt of some style.

Evidence of land use for the main, central farm comes from this early survey, which exists now only as a tracing. It covers the 186 acres which Sir Robert Croke was about to sell to William Eldridge. The Bourne Stream which bisects the farm is clearly shown with the Pond Bays, into which the former iron masters had dammed it, now being meadows. On the whole the land to the north of Postern Lane was meadow or pasture while that to the south was under the plough.

The proportions of land use were:

	per cent
arable	55.4
meadow	33.3
pasture	11.2
hops	0.2

The small hopgarden was near the house.

This was, therefore, a mixed farm. The best soil would be concentrated near the watercourses, and it would change to clay as it rose towards the south.

The documents do not allow identification of the other farms with any certainty, but they too would enjoy good alluvial soil to the north near the River, and heavier, more difficult soils to the south.

Tenants and leases in the eighteenth century

Farming leases are not commonly found, so the nine that exist for our three farms are of some interest. Three are for the Cage, three for the Stair and three for a 56-acre parcel at the Postern known as Hooker's. The last three, starting in 1725, are not all within our period, but are included for comparison. The concern here is with tenants, with the duration of the lease, the end-term provision, rents and any special covenants.

A factor of great importance is continuity of tenure and its effect on productivity. It is debatable whether the length of the term, or even the existence of a written lease, is indicative of security of tenure. Many farmers over the country held their leasehold from generation to generation without formal agreements.[10] Yet, at the time of writing, the National Farmers' Union, opposing the government's wish to enforce shorter leases, is saying that farmers need at least 15 years' security of tenure to be able to farm properly. Farmers will say that only continuity over generations will give a man knowledge and experience of his soil's possibilities.[11]

Provision for land to be left fertile and not overused for several years before the expiry of the lease was seen as important, and there are some differences in the conditions included for this. After all, it might be the landlord himself who decided to take the land in hand.

Nowhere is individual policy seen to be more varied than with rents. This was apparently a feature in Kent. In 1805 John Boys wrote that rents varied surprisingly from farm to farm, but that the average seemed to be about 15s per acre.[12]

The Cage

John Simmons took the lease of the Cage in 1733, succeeding Robert Oliver. The Simmons family appears to have held leasehold land at Larkhale (Larkhall) in Hadlow, and to have owned the land we have seen called Winchester Farm near the Stair. His Cage lease was to run for 31 years, an exceptionally long term.[13] In 1766 his son Robert took it over and now the term was reduced to 21 years. In fact, Alchin, the owner, had to relet after 16 years, presumedly on the death of Robert. The two sons, Robert and William succeeded their father, but Robert soon disappears from the documents.

William Simmons played a full part in Parish affairs and was known to the Woodgates. In a letter of 1788 one of their ladies wrote that George 'Boorne' had 'engag'd a large building for Mr. Simmons at the Cage.'[14] In fact family alliances connected William closely with both the gentry and superior tradesmen in the locality. He married into the Alchins, and was uncle to Thomas Marin, landowner of Hextall House. This was through his sister's marriage into that family. Another sister, Ann, married a Cheesman who was probably of a Hadlow yeoman family. A third sister, Sarah, married John Mugridge, a Tonbridge tallowchandler who, as we shall see later, was the prosperous head of a rising family.

The first lease, of 1733, penalised the tenant if he ploughed pasture within seven years of termination. This was an unusually long end-term and Alchin's lease reduced this to three years.

Special covenants concerned the meadows purchased by Hooper. In 1733 the tenant was expected to maintain access between the Cage and Buddles Mead beyond the Hadlow Road. In 1766 Robert Simmons was required to build a new weir with floodgates in 'that part of the Stream that runs in the Lower Mead adjacent the Other Mead belonging to North Frith Estate'. This was meadow formerly called Common or East Mead.

The rents of the three leases work out at 5s per acre in 1733, and 8s for both 1766 and 1782. This would seem to be low.

The Stair

Tenure here was not continuous. In 1744 Samuel Mills senior leased the Farm to Richard Lomas, yeoman of Hadlow, for 13 years, but after 10 years he seems to have renegotiated, while maintaining the term.[15] Subsequently, there was a period when Mills took the Farm in hand, a practice of owners who were confident that they could get good prices. Then, in 1785, a new tenant was found. This was Richard Larkin, a Tonbridge yeoman. His lease was for 15 years. The 1754 lease was conditional upon Lomas living in the farmhouse, presumably to prevent subletting. Larkin could sublet only with permission.

The rent was raised only slightly over the three leases. It was set at £54 for the first two, but payment in 1754 was to be supplemented in kind by the addition of ten bushels of apples. The rent per acre works out at 18s. In 1785 this rose to 19s 9d. But there was one hidden extra. In 1744 it was proposed to build a new Oast. Instead of the tenant being responsible for the building and the owner finding the materials, here the rent was increased by £6 to cover the costs.

Hooker's, Postern

This was previously known as Gilbert's and was probably part of the present Postern Park, to the north and east of the central Postern

Farm. The site had included a house, garden, orchard and outbuild-ings, plus ten pieces of arable, meadow and pasture, and six pieces of 'meadow or Island ground'. In 1725 Peter Zinzan leased to James Eldridge for 15 years. In 1740 John Hooker renewed the lease but this time for only seven years.[16]

After a gap of 14 years (presumably one lease is missing), Hooker renewed once more, but there are now differences. The first two leases had mentioned that the owner intended to build a new house and barn but the 1754 lease omits this. Also, in the last lease the acreage has been increased from 56 to 70. The term is now for 21 years.

The rents are more in line with those of the Stair than of the Cage. For the original 56 acres in 1725 it was £42 (to be paid to George Hooper). In 1754 the rent had risen to £50, an increase from 15s to 19s per acre.

Summary

Although some covenants in these nine leases are routinely found, there are others which reveal the close interest taken by owners. In general, it is the Stair that shows this more than the two large farms.

For the Cage and Hooker's, the tenant families held the leasehold over two or three generations and would seem eventually to have acquired the site or to have married into the owning family. At the Stair little is known of the tenants, who do not appear to have had family connections with each other or adjacent parishes, and most held either freeholds or leaseholds in addition to our farms.

End-term provision was always laid down despite the hereditary nature of the leases. It took the form of safeguarding some of the land from overcultivation by ensuring that it was left as pasture or sown with clover.

Regarding rents, the leases for Hooker's are not strictly comparable with the others as they are mostly earlier. What can be said is that in the middle of the century Hooker fixed a rent of 19s per acre, Alchin one of 8s and Mills one of 18s. Over the following thirty years the rents for the Cage and the Stair rose slightly. Even allowing for the difficulty of working the soil at the Cage, this farm seems to have been leased for an exceptionally low sum.

Special covenants do occur but are not of great moment. The rent of the Stair was increased to the tune of ten bushels of fruit, a useful addition to a townsman's apple store. A surcharge of £6 to cover the cost of building a new Oast was perhaps more significant. Protection against flooding was of concern to all riparian owners and it is no surprise to find Alchin anxious about the building of a weir.

The descent of the properties

The Cage and Starvecrow

Two families of lawyers practising in the Town were closely linked both by marriage and by ownership of these two areas. They were the Hoopers and the Alchins. George Hooper, attorney, lived at Lyons and owned, also, Cockhammons in Mill Lane, besides other properties in the Town, and lands in several Kentish parishes, totalling in all about 700 acres. Hooper had bought the Cage in 1697 and Starvecrow in 1714. It can be presumed that, with such an amount of real estate, Hooper would have counted in this small town among the gentry, and would have taken a central part in communal life. Two examples of his involvement can be found in the Will he made in 1742. The Parish Church was to have a 'Water Engine' and the officers of the Court Leet were to have 20 shillings 'for wine for their accommodation at the Rose and Crown'.

George Hooper left the Cage to his son George, and other property eventually to his younger son, Stephen. He named his brother-in-law as Trustee, and this was George Alchin.[17]

The brother of George the elder was Stephen and he died childless after making his Will in 1747. He turned to the Alchin family as his beneficiaries, leaving considerable property in the Southborough area to his nephew and namesake, Stephen-Hooper Alchin. When George Hooper the younger came to make his Will twelve years later it seems that his family were already deceased, and he, too, benefited the Alchin sons. The elder, George was to have the Cage and Stephen-Hooper was to have Starvecrow. No doubt because he was already enjoying his Southborough inheritance, Stephen-Hooper soon sold Starvecrow to his brother.[18]

This George Alchin followed his father in becoming an attorney. He continued to lease the Cage to the Simmons family as has been seen, but Starvecrow he leased separately. Frog Mead, near Frog Bridge over the Pen Stream, had already been leased to Thomas Mills, a younger son of Samuel who owned the Stair, and Alchin chose to extend his lease to include Starvecrow.

From 1759 until late in the following century, the Cage and Starvecrow continued in the hands of Alchins or collaterals. Whether George Alchin remained in Tonbridge is doubtful, as the family seem to have had strong connections with West Malling, and in his Will of 1785 he is styled as 'of West Malling, attorney'.[19] He named as his executor his 'good tenant' William Simmons, and in 1804 his widow, Frances, strengthened the relationship by marrying William. The Cage did not come into Simmons' hands, however, for, when Frances died, her daughter, another Frances, inherited it, apparently together with Starvecrow. Her sister, who lived in West Malling, was to have a rent charge from Starvecrow. In 1827 Frances died and bequeathed both farms to a nephew of her stepfather, William Simmons. This nephew was Thomas Martin, of Hextall House, East Peckham. Martin was a large landowner, holding lands in Hadlow, Tudeley and Tonbridge. He was Lay Rector of Hadlow Church. His uncle Simmons had already died, leaving him the small Pot Kiln Farm near Hilden Bridge, which he had purchased at the turn of the century.

By 1838 Martin had installed a bailiff at the Cage, while he held Starvecrow in hand together with other land towards Higham Green. His heir was Edwin Martin, but it seems that he moved his family away from West Kent.

Summary
The Cage with its adjacent farm and meadowland, passed through centuries of ownership by one family and its branches. The earlier members, the Hoopers and the Alchins, were lawyers practising

either in the Town or in Malling. We know that both Hoopers and Alchins were servants to the Manor of Tonbridge as Clerks to the Lord's Courts, and were also Clerks to the Parish Vestry, and legal advisors to many of the local gentry, farmers and tradesmen. They were owners of considerable real estate which in itself would have given them gentry status.

Relationships with their tenants were probably always good, as indicated by the lengthy leases to the Simmons family, as well as the low rent they charged.

All the evidence points to a steady and continuous rise in the fortunes of the Simmons-Martin family. Simmons acquired a house in the Town as well as the small farm, he married well, as did his sisters, and he extended his house. His success will be parallelled slightly later by the rise of the Mugridges, particularly William, from the beginning of the nineteenth century, as will appear. Thomas Martin benefited from the inheritance of a childless uncle's estate in the same way as the Alchin brothers inherited from both their father and their childless uncle.

The Parsonage/Yardley House

In 1754 The Parsonage, with other lands, was settled on the new bride of Dan Groombridge for her jointure. How the Farm came into Groombridge hands is unknown, but the family was long established in the Town and of some considerable stature.

From the seventeenth century Groombridges had owned a house on the west of the High Street, towards the present Bank Street. Nearby were a slaughterhouse, a hog pound and 'a wood lodge and yards'. In this house Dan's grandfather of the same name had lived, and no doubt his father, John, had been brought up there. Nearby lived James Norris, carpenter, and he was witness to the grandfather's Will of 1748 (proved 1751).[20]

Despite these trading connections, both the grandfather and his two grandsons, John and Dan, styled themselves as 'gentlemen' so it is worth delving further into their background.

Dan senior is recorded in the 1736 Quarter Sessions Books as being responsible for reporting to the Justices on the state of the Great Bridge and recommending a man suitable to carry out repairs.[21] This confirms that the grandfather was an attorney, ranking, therefore, with the lesser gentry. As the Will of Dan II refers to his 'law papers, law books, presentments and manuscript books' we can assume that he continued the legal practice. Dan II had attended Tonbridge School in the 1730s.

Turning to marriage connections and family settlements, the evidence of wealth and standing becomes even more convincing. The bride of 1754 was Philadelphia Baker, daughter of George Baker Esq. of Mayfield. The style 'Esquire' signified that he was the son of one of the landed gentry. Her portion was a handsome £1,000. Dan's wealth or prospects must have been promising to attract such a sum. In fact, his background was prestigious, not to say flamboyant.

John Groombridge I, father of John and Dan, had died before the grandfather so it fell to the elder Dan to safeguard the interests of his daughter-in-law and her two sons.

This daughter-in-law was Margaret Rivers, herself of a substantial family. Hasted tells us that a branch of her family was settled in Hadlow and at one time had owned Fish Hall, but Margaret was the daughter of Sir George Rivers of Chafford Place, near Penshurst. Sir George had no male issue at the time of his death in 1734, but he had five legitimate and seven illegitimate daughters[22]. After a nine-year dispute over the inheritance, Margaret received £1,050 as her share. Dan Groombridge I invested this money on her behalf not in land but in the stock of the South Sea Company. This was not as foolhardy a venture as it might have been earlier in the century. The Bank of England, together with the South Sea and East India Companies, was much involved in upholding the government in the 1740s. The success at the Battle of Dettingen in 1742 had inspired 'patriotic bellicosity', which led to a general desire among the gentry to support the National Debt. Financially, investors could feel reasonably confident.[23]

When Dan came to write his Will in a clear hand and practical style in 1748, he explained that John, his eldest grandson, had, at his marriage, been entitled to half this stock but that Dan had chosen not to sell it, but to borrow £650 on his securities, and to let John have that. Dan, the younger grandson, was to inherit the stock, with accrued interest, and to repay the £650 out of it. The grandsons also shared Dan's real estate – a farm of 60 acres in Tudeley, and another in Hayesden, as well as property in the Town. The Parsonage was omitted from the Will, but this could be normal practice with settled land. It would descend to the use of the widow, Philadelphia, while she remained unmarried, and then to the use of any children.

Events now moved fast. John II had married, as we saw, before 1748 and set up as a linen-draper in Maidstone. But, surprisingly neither John, nor Dan lived long after marriage and neither had any children. Dan was the first to die, in the winter of 1756-7. He made his brother his heir. John died a few years later, his Will being proved in 1762.[24] His widow, therefore, inherited all the Groombridge estate except the Parsonage.

By 1766 both these widows, Philadelphia and Mary, were remarried, Philadelphia to a London merchant, and Mary to Henry Goodwyn, a gentleman of Blackheath. In 1801 Henry Goodwyn 'of Maze Hill, Greenwich', took out a mortgage on the Parsonage with a John Milles 'of St. Sepulchre's, Middlesex, druggist.' The mortgage took the form of a conveyance to the use of the mortgagee for the sum of '£1,211, to the use of the mortgagor for 500 years.'[25]

Goodwyn died in 1816 and it would seem that, the following year, Milles, who by now lived in Tonbridge, came into full possession of the Parsonage, by assignment to him 'in Trust to Attend the Inheritance.' He straightway sold off the four-acre piece on the far side of the Shipbourne Road to James-Eldridge West who was in process of aggregating his lands at Dry Hill, Hilden and Cage Green.

Although John Milles continued to rent out the Parsonage, his connections were all local. His name pervades the Parish documents over the next twenty years. There seems to be a link between John Milles the chemist and John Milles (Millus or Millis) the farmer. In the 1820s a Milles was tenant of Bourne Mill and Fish Lodge farms near Somerhill. In 1825 John Milles senior and junior served as

Parish Officers. So the probability is that the son, having established himself in London on the fringe of the rising medical profession, had returned to settle in Tonbridge, and invest in land. By 1838 he was the tenant of Walter's Farm to the west of the Postern. In the early 1830s Milles sold the Parsonage and the new owner demolished the farmhouse to build Yardley House slightly to the south of it.

From now on the property was owned by the gentry who developed the grounds with a Lodge on the Shipbourne Road. The 1841 Census shows a Frances Shaw apparently running a school there, while by 1849 George Nottidge, a magistrate and landed proprietor, had taken it over. His extended family and their servants numbered 19 altogether.

Summary
The Groombridges, as Town-dwelling professional men, used the Parsonage as settled land which could be sold only by family agreement. Like the Hooper-Alchins they owned considerable land elsewhere and, to judge from John's marriage into the Rivers family, they were accepted into the gentry class at least by the 1730s.

Descent passed through a collateral to a widow, soon remarried. Whether her husband sold in order to buy land nearer his main holding, or to solve financial problems, is unclear. It is probable that the man who lent the £1,200 to Goodwyn and ended by owning the property, was one of the many medical men whose status, like that of many scriveners (conveyancers) and attorneys, was higher by about 1780 and would continue to rise. By associating to secure corporately agreed standards and, later, qualifications, this group, always evident in Tonbridge, was becoming assured of a 'respectable' standing.[26]

Stair Farm
The descent of the Stair in some ways parallels that of the Parsonage. Each was held for about half a century by one man residing in Tonbridge Town and leasing out, and each was just a small part of the owner's total estate. But the Stair was a viable farm and the Mills family was more involved with farming and its products than the

Groombridges. Each property was sold in the early years of the nineteenth century to men already known in Tonbridge, but drawing part of their income, it would seem, from London enterprises. But there the parallels end, as the Mills family were so large that some could not be expected to inherit land, and had to leave the Parish. Some had to struggle to maintain their standing.

Samuel Mills senior had inherited Stair Place, new-built in 1733, from his uncle Samuel Vandelure. His inheritance also included land near Higham Green and in East Peckham. Both men were traders in the Town, Vandelure a mercer, and Mills a miller.

Five years after inheriting, Samuel married Elizabeth Walter and they had at least nine children – Samuel, George, Thomas, John, Elizabeth, William, Vandelure, Henry and Mary, most of whom lived to at least middle age. Although this must have been a drain on his resources, Samuel sent the boys to Tonbridge School in the 1740s and 1750s. We know that Samuel II and Thomas, and possibly Vandelure, became yeomen locally, and can assume that it was Samuel who inherited Stair. George became an attorney in Sevenoaks, John took up the hosiery trade in London, William entered the Church and Eliza married a papermaker.

In 1780 Samuel senior styled himself as 'gentleman', a title becoming more common by then, and he was certainly substantial. The Land Tax returns for that year show him owning 15 properties in or near the Town, including the house occupied by his eldest son, a slaughterhouse and the Rose and Crown. Samuel II owned three properties including Medway Wharf. Together their holdings were more numerous than those of any other man except the Lord of the Manor. Samuel I held shares in the Medway Navigation Company and in a Turnpike Trust.

During the year before he died, Samuel drew up his own account of his annual income from property rents, and the interest from his shares. The whole amounted to just under £390, and the largest amounts came from his 'River Shares' – £66, Little Mills, East Peckham – £50, and 'The Crown Inn' – £40. The rest came in small amounts from a total of 22 sources.[27]

However, there were many calls on his wealth. His son, George, was made bankrupt in 1790 and the father advanced him £300. The portion for his daughter Eliza on her marriage to William Stidolph, papermaker of Chafford, was the generous sum of £800. But Stidolph was declared bankrupt in 1786, thirty years later, and Eliza had to move with him and their three daughters to Camberwell. Samuel by then was well into his eighties so the needy members of the family could harbour expectations. Samuel made his Will in 1791 and died the following year. He left specified household goods for George and Thomas, and some houses in East Lane for the benefit of Eliza, but the bulk of his real estate was to be shared out 'as Equal as you can amongst yourselves.'[28] There was no mention of his eldest son, Samuel, nor of the Stair, but there is some evidence that it was held jointly for a while.

Inevitably many of the houses were sold over the following few years, and there was in some cases considerable bitterness felt by the poorer children about delays, about legal fees, and about the fairness of the ensuing apportionments. When Eliza came to die in 1803 the elder sons who were Executors had to contact descendants in America and each received only small sums from the sale of her inheritance.

The Stair must have been sold during the first two decades of the nineteenth century, but we know for certain only that, by 1820, it had come into the possession of James-Eldridge West of the Postern and Dry Hill. We saw him aggregating to the west of the Shipbourne Road. Now he was acquiring land to the north of Postern Park, still his father's house. At about this time West's tenant at Postern House, William Mugridge, held the farm adjacent to the Stair. This was now known as Winchester, and, as we noted, had at one time been held by the Simmons family. Mugridge died in the 1840s and during that decade West acquired Winchester, whether by purchase or inheritance is unknown. This made, with the Stair, a 140-acre holding of varied soils and gradients.[29]

Summary

Unfortunately, there is little evidence, apart from leases, to link Stair with its owners. However, the history of the Mills family, and that of the later owners, Mugridge and West, is well documented.

The Mills family had difficulties, which must have beset many at the time of the French Wars. This is the largest family of sons that we meet in our study. Also, the elder Samuel Mills lived for almost 60 years in the enjoyment of his estate. The process of sharing this out from 1791 was long, and for some, bitter.

After the Mills' departure, ownership of Stair and Winchester is unclear. The latter may have been held by William Eldridge before passing to William Mugridge and then to James E West. The Hadlow Tithe regards the two farms as one unit.

By the time of West's death in 1851 he held an almost continuous swathe of land to the East of Tonbridge and a similar swathe to the west.

The Tanyard

As with the last two properties, one family held this site for most of the eighteenth century and sold in the first two decades of the nineteenth. Until 1768 this was the Twort family, and then followed a collateral branch named Eldridge. But this was a more modest property than the previous ones, and its owners held only small amounts of land in addition. The Tworts were tanners, and a junior branch of yeomen stock in Horsmonden.

Harry Twort had working with him in the first half of the century his son Harry and a Thomas Twort who may have been either another son or a nephew. Harry senior held a farm in Seal and two houses in the Town which he let out. When his son Harry married in 1713, the Tanyard was settled on the couple as counter to Elizabeth's portion of £400.[30] This was a goodly portion, typical of superior yeomen families at that time, especially considering that she was one of six siblings.

Robert Oliver, her father, owned farms in Shipbourne, Hadlow, Tudeley and Frant but he was also tenant of the Cage. A further complication was that the farm he owned in Hadlow was leased to Harry Twort senior. As with the Alchins and the Simmons family, so with the Olivers and the Tworts, the landlord-tenant relationship was close socially.

By 1744 Harry II and Elizabeth had not had children, so they drew up an agreement that the Tanyard should go to Henry Eldridge, Elizabeth's nephew and Harry's godson. It is likely that Twort had supervised Henry's apprenticeship. Richard Filmer quotes an unnamed writer of 1752 who describes tanning as 'a genteelish business'. Strong lads needed to be brought up in it. He goes on to stress the lengthy nature of such an apprenticeship. 'A master cannot well set up in it under a capital of £500.'[31]

The Eldridge connection is interesting because it reveals a link with the Postern Eldridges who were themselves yeomen at this time. Elizabeth's sister had married a Christopher Eldridge and her two boys were Henry and William. We cannot identify this Christopher for certain, but a seventeenth century yeoman of that name farmed in Bidborough and held land on which Mabledon was to be built. He was the father of William who settled at the Postern in 1678. As mentioned earlier in this book (pp. 73-4), a later Christopher Eldridge (1701-99) farmed off Quarry Hill.

Harry Twort senior made his Will in 1762 when he must have been over eighty. He made elaborate arrangements for Elizabeth, his daughter-in-law, to have a £10 rent charge from the Seal Farm and the two houses in the Town, while he could now afford to make a money bequest of £300 to his son, Harry, as well as allowing him the remaining rents and profits from these holdings which were to be held in Trust by the Tworts of Horsmonden and eventually to come fully into their hands.

Only six years later, in 1768, Harry junior himself died. In his Will he confirmed the settlement of the Tanyard on his godson after his widow's death, but added a proviso that if he were to marry, he must seek the approval of his aunt, or he would have to share the Tanyard with his brother and two cousins. This was a not uncommon constraint. We find that the Horsmonden Tworts were similarly anxious about the behaviour of their children. A grandfather there laid down in his Will that his granddaughters were 'to be brought up in a devout and proper manner.'

Henry Eldridge, who was already 'occupying' the Tanyard, had to wait 24 years before taking it over from his aunt, and it took him several years after his uncle's death to find an acceptable bride. She was Susannah Wray, daughter of a tanner in Offham, and her portion was no more than £300, but as their family grew up Henry was able to purchase an additional ten acres of meadow and hopground adjacent to the Tanyard. He also built a new house beside Sanguins before his eldest son, George-Wray, married in 1809. There was a second son, William, and the Tanyard was early settled on them both, but the arrangement was that, on Henry's death, William, an ironmonger, should sell out to his brother for £1,100. (The trustee for this 1790 agreement was Samuel Mills.) Meanwhile Henry and George-Wray appear to have worked together, and they took out a mortgage on both houses and the Tanyard for £700.

George-Wray and his wife had six children who were baptised by the Methodist Minister from the Sevenoaks Circuit. So far the family seem thoroughly well established and respectable members of the local community.[32]

But money was short. In 1813 father and son sought to raise more by mortgaging six of the ten acres of meadow. The interest on the first loan had been repaid but not the capital, and the original lender was demanding repayment in full. A Tonbridge farmer was found to pay off the capital and to advance a further £1,300. But this served only to tide them over, it seems, for upon the death of Henry around 1820, George-Wray sold up. He died in Maidstone, in 1832.

The new owner was of the Waite family. In the early years of the eighteenth century we find Waites renting part of the Trench Area. The name is common in our Parish, but it may be no coincidence that Harry Twort's two houses in the Town were let to two ladies named 'Wait.' The John Waite who had now bought the Tanyard was the brother of William who owned Loampits, just to the north. Their father owned Fish Hall at this time. John paid £4,000 for the

Tanyard, its two houses and fourteen acres. (We note that William Eldridge's half share had been valued at £1,100 at the turn of the century.) John paid by instalments over five years. He remained in possession at least until 1840.

We have no way of assessing his standing, except that he was styled 'gentleman'. Roy Porter groups tanners together with merchants, innkeepers, millers, and butchers, as some of those belonging to what he calls 'the commercial middle-class.'[33]

Summary

The Twort-Eldridges may have been more isolated, more self-contained than, say, the Simmons or the Mugridge families. The name Harry Twort appears among the lists of Parish Officers for only three separate years – 1733, 1754 and 1769 – while our other middling families served continuously over several generations. Their names are not found in the legal documents of other local families. They married within a small circle of yeomen or fellow-tanners, and the Horsmonden Tworts exerted a considerable influence on the Tonbridge tanners, both using the legal services of the Scoones.

Their real estate seems to have contracted with the loss of the farm in Seal and their financial situation seems to have worsened, like that of the Goodwyns, from the time of the French Wars. In the tanners' Wills there is no mention of investments, nor of any London connections.

The Postern Area

As we have already seen, the early picture of the descent of the various farms at the Postern, and of the homesteads, is blurred. We have chosen to follow the Eldridge-Wests even although we cannot state with certainty which was the land they owned in the eighteenth century, or how they expanded.

A significant date was 1757, when James Eldridge married Mary Whitaker. (It may be relevant that, as Savills, the house agents have said, Postern House was built in that year.) Who was this Eldridge?

His grandfather was William, yeoman, of Bidborough, the son of the Christopher Eldridge, yeoman, already met, a scion of several branches of the family. As the Postern Eldridges throughout our period retained lands in the Southborough area, we can presume that these were inherited from this William. He bought the main, central farm at the Postern in 1678 and soon added to it 17 acres adjoining the Old Forge once occupied by John Goldfinch.[34]

William's two sons, John and James, grew up as neighbours of Augustine Taylor, tenant-farmer of 140 acres on the Postern. James, in his Will of 1742 (he died much later) left a small legacy to one of the Taylor daughters.[35] In 1728 John, William's eldest son, bought the farm that Taylor had occupied and thereafter the Poor Rate assessments charged him for 'Taylor's' and 'Goldfinch's', among other pieces unnamed.[36]

While John owned and occupied his 140 acres and more, James leased 56 acres from the Lord of the Manor of Tonbridge. It may well be that, when the last Hooker left the Town in 1793, a descendant of James acquired this farming unit. Another small piece of land at the Postern was still held by a member of a gentry family until about this time. This was a little meadow originally part of Great Amours (Amos) Mead. This six-acre piece had been sold off to Thomas Weller soon after William Eldridge had acquired the Postern central farm, and was handed down through the Weller family for several generations as settled land, until 1800. Then it was sold back to the Eldridges, this time to another William.

Returning to the two brothers, John and James, sons of William I, we know that John had paid £3,468 for his 140 acres in 1728. He had four sons – James, John, William and Thomas, but his brother was childless. The four sons of John, therefore, stood to gain from both their father's and their uncle's Wills. In the uncle's Will the eldest son, James, was left 'my farm and the lands usually letten therewith' but these are not named. The other sons were bequeathed either money or lands elsewhere. In the father's Will only William is mentioned, so we presume that lifetime provision had been made for the others. To William he left 50 acres of Postern land. This Will was made in 1759 and names John's brother James as Trustee. It seems likely that both John and James, the father and the uncle, died in the early 1760s and that James had good expectations when he married in 1757.

His bride was Mary, the granddaughter of Thomas Whitaker, at one time Sheriff, and Lord of the Manor of Trottiscliffe. He left land in the Cage Green area and houses in the Town which she brought to James, the yeoman-farmer, who would thus seem to have made a good match. He and Mary had only one child, Amy (or Emma). When she came to marry she seems to have made an even better match. The groom, in 1782, was John Hartrup West, a second-generation Blackfriars merchant. The Revd G W Woodgate links him with a family of Hartrups who have local connections.[37] Certainly the name Hartrup (Hartup or Hartnup) appears frequently among farmers and clergy in the area. John and Amy lived at Postern Park and had one son, James-Eldridge, before Amy died. For several years John remained a widower while his son, 'the tall handsome Captain' with the speech affectation, was growing up and becoming an Officer in the Militia. Then John married Maria Woodgate, a younger daughter of William of Somerhill. Socialising occurred between the Wests, the Woodgates, the Allnutts of Leigh and the Nouailles of Sevenoaks. When Henry Woodgate of Riverhill died, leaving a daughter, the Wests became her guardians and employed a governess for her at £100 per annum.

Meanwhile James-Eldridge married into the Ashburnham family, bought Dry Hill Lodge, (the present Manor House) and brought up a large family, the sons doing well at Tonbridge School and entering the professions.

James, John and William Eldridge probably died around the turn of the century for the Poor Rate Assessments now charge only two men for the whole Postern Area – John H West and a William Mugridge. From the Tithe Award of 1838 it is clear that Mugridge was a tenant, and he will merit special attention later.

John H West played a full part in Town and County affairs. He was called upon to act as assignee for the estate of William Francis Woodgate, bankrupted in 1815, but, to judge from his purchases of land, he himself suffered little at this time of hardship. He and his son were developing estates to the west of the Town. They acquired parts of Hilden, had inherited Cage Green Farm, and James was to buy Dry Hill Lodge and, later, the Castle, where he lived for a time. As far as is known, John H West continued to live at Postern Park, but at the time of his death in 1836 he mentions that he was employing a bailiff. By his Will James inherited all his father's real estate. The personal estate totalled £1,004. To his wife he left a large and sumptuous collection of books, furniture, silverware and china. The egg-stand, 'sallat spoons', asparagus tongs, pictures and pianoforte, diamond earrings, and elegant furniture are all proudly detailed.[38]

When James-Eldridge came to make his Will in 1851 his personal estate was in excess of £7,000. His real estate makes an impressive list: Stemp's Farm, Southborough, the whole of the Postern, Stair and Winchester, parts of the Hilden Estate, Cage Green Farm, Dry Hill, some houses in the Town and lands in Hadlow and Tudeley.[39]

After 1836 there were no Wests in residence at the Postern. Besides William Mugridge who lived at Postern House, there were three tenant farmers, John Hatch at Postern Park, John Chatfield at the central Postern Farm, including the Old Forge and Postern Heath House, and Jesse Chatfield at Upper Postern. We know that the Hatch family farmed in Tudeley in the previous century, and that there were Chatfields at the Trench at that time also.

Summary

It would seem that it took the whole of the eighteenth century for the Eldridges to take over the entire Postern area. They were, in general, long-lived men with small families. Above all, they were living on the spot.

Relationships between them and the tenants on the Area seem to have been good, especially between the Taylor's and James Eldridge, and between William Mugridge and James E West. It is likely that social distinctions between landlords and tenants tended to be blurred.

It may have been the injection of mercantile wealth which advanced the standing of the Eldridge-Wests after the 1782 marriage, while gifts from, and the patronage of, the high-spending Woodgates, would soon have established the Wests among the more respected gentry of the area.

From the end of the Napoleonic Wars to his death nearly 40 years later, James E West pursued a policy of land purchase on both sides of the Town as well as of residences within it. His total acreage did not, of course, rival that of the superior gentry in West Kent, and the division of his real estate among his six children must have left each with but a modest inheritance. However, the sons had gained qualifications for the professions, so that rents were for them a secondary income.

The three Postern farms were all leased out during the first half of the nineteenth century, a development which reversed the trend of the previous one. The incoming tenants were descendants of wellknown local farming families.

William Mugridge, Gentleman?

The 1841 Census distinguishes between farmers and those of independent means, and classes Mugridge with the former. In legal documents, where he appears frequently as attesting the deeds of the superior 'middling sort', he is styled as a 'gentleman'. He seems to be a classic example of the socially prospering commercial middle-class, to be compared with William Simmons in the eighteenth century. It may be that he had still a little way to advance before he would be accepted on an equal footing with the gentry.

It is possible to follow three generations of the Mugridge family in Tonbridge. In 1734 the first William married Susan Cockerton from East Anglia. She brought him a third share in a farm in Essex and two houses.[40] The Mugridges were tallowchandlers who owned two houses with a plot running between the High Street and the Churchyard. One of the houses contained a shop. They also owned, under the Manor, eight acres of land off Quarry Hill, the site of the Woodside Road development. This piece of land was called Coldshotts. It faced north.

The links with East Anglia continued after the marriage. One of

William's sons was a mercer in Norfolk, and, by the time William made his Will in 1765, he owned three more houses plus seven acres of land in Essex. He had at that time three sons and three daughters. Two of his sons were to inherit the Essex properties while to John came the chandling business and Coldshotts. (Neighbours in the High Street were George Bourne, the builder, who leased from Samuel Mills, and James Norris, the carpenter who was William's brother-in-law and who did construction work for the Medway Navigation Company.) Mugridge's three daughters were each to have a portion of £300 on marriage.

In 1772 John married Sarah Simmons, daughter of William of Hadlow and probably of the Cage. Her sisters had portions of £300 each, so we presume that Sarah herself brought that sum to John. Thirty years later, John made his Will, and he had obviously prospered. He bequeathed to his son, William, 'gentleman' of the Postern, the two Town houses and Coldshotts. Out of the rents he was to pay his cousin Thomas an annuity of £250. There then followed money bequests totalling the surprising sum of £7,650. To this son, also, John left his shares in the Medway Navigation Company.

How William had acquired the House and gardens at the Postern, and also the farm known as Winchester with a small parcel off Three Elm Lane, is a mystery, but the latter is labelled on a map as 'Late William Eldridge'. Can we presume a link by marriage, when we also find in a Manorial rental of 1802, that an unnamed messuage 'descended' to Mugridge after the death of William Eldridge?[41]

In the early years of the nineteenth century, Will was admitted into the social circle of the Wests and Woodgates, although perhaps on sufferance. One of the lady Woodgates wrote of 'Will Mugridge and Harper' going to dances at Greentrees with the local gentry – they were 'agreeable people, but not good dancers'.

By 1838, if not before, the Stair and Winchester were in the owner-occupancy of Mugridge, and this unit must have been sublet. He retained his shares in the Navigation Company and bought some in the Gas Company newly established in 1836. In the 1841 Census we discover him living at the Postern with his cousin, Thomas – two old men attended by three servants. He died in the early 1840s after long years of involvement with Parish affairs.

Perhaps he was called 'farmer' because he worked the Stair and Winchester, and 'gentleman' because he resided in style at the Postern. We could call him an example of upward and outward mobility.

The properties in 1838

The Tithe Awards and Maps of about 1838 are valuable in that they show field names and sizes, and cropping, although the assessors were naturally not interested in stock or in commercial or industrial usage of the land.[42]

The Cage
The names and sizes of the fields remained virtually unchanged from 1767. The Pen Meads are now called Great and Little Meads. A rough analysis of cropping in 1838 shows that arable predominated as it did in the earlier period. Pasture, fruit and hops have not yet grown in significance.

Land use at the Cage, 1838		Land use at Starvecrow with the meadows, 1838	
	per cent		per cent
arable	52.6	woodland	35.8
meadow	22.2	pasture	35.0
woodland	10.2	meadow	21.7
arable with hops	6.8	arable	6.7
pasture	4.7		
orchard	3.4		

The Hadlow Tithe particulars combine the eastern part of Starvecrow with the meadows over the Hadlow Road. All this was held in hand by Thomas Martin, together with land near Higham Green which we have not included in this study.

Although Martin was leasing out the Cage, the whole area that he owned can be seen to form units which complement each other if the farming is overviewed.

189

The Parsonage/Yardley

In the Tithe Award the name of the site is given as 'Parsonage' while the dwelling is called 'Yardley House.' On the Map the building is square in plan, situated immediately to the south of an L-shaped building, which may well be the remains of the old Parsonage Farm. A lodge stands on Shipbourne Road at the end of the driveway which runs beside the 'Slip' or shaw. This drive subsequently became Yardley Park Road.

To the south of the drive is Church Meadow, unchanged since 1754 when Dan Groombridge arranged his marriage settlement. In addition there are just three meadows totalling six acres, a small orchard and a filbert (nut) plantation.

The whole must have presented as a pleasant semirural and salubrious retreat, laid out perhaps more stylishly but still to the pattern of 1750.

Stair and Winchester

The Tithe Map for Hadlow is faint, but the Award shows that Stair and Winchester, both at this time held in hand by Will Mugridge, were run as one unit of 188 acres.

Land use at Stair and Winchester

	per cent
arable	41.3
meadow	16.8
arable and hops	14.7
pasture	12.5
hops	9.3
orchard	2.7
woodland	2.7

There was considerably less woodland here than at the Cage. The small amount of fruitgrowing is surprising in view of the eighteenth century owner's insistence on fruit as part-payment of rent.

In general it is still a mixed farm with hops now featuring significantly.

The Tanyard

We saw that it was Henry Eldridge, at the turn of the century, who purchased ten additional acres to square off the original four-acre site, and who built a new house (perhaps the core of the present Grove House) as an addition to Sanguins. By 1838 there seem to have been no more developments, except that the dwellings are now described as 'House and Cottages.'

As well as the usual gardens and orchard adjoining the nucleus of seven buildings, the newly purchased fields still consist of about six acres of meadow and a four-acre hop garden. This last, still known as 'Gunnings', remains in shape and usage exactly as it was in 1699.

The Postern Area

The original central Postern Farm of 186 acres as shown on the survey of 1674-5 can be identified as the core of the Postern Farm of the Tithe. Two thirds of the fields retain their names, sizes and usage. A few have been divided in two. The Pond Bay Meadows have been combined together as Bay Field, but that is still meadowland. There is still a hopgarden and orchard near the homesteads.

But there are two changes which alter the nature of this farm. One is that it has increased in size to 212 acres with the absorption of meadows near Postern Bridge. (We saw that Amos Mead had regained its small six-acre part by about 1800.) The other is the merging of six fields to the south on the rising ground towards Somerhill. These had been arable in 1674/5 but now they form one 42-acre Paddock. There is some evidence from a preliminary Ordnance Survey Map of 1799 that this merger had already taken place by this date.[43] The need for the production of extra wheat during the French Wars, and the high prices being paid for it, could have caused the grubbing up of some hedgerows. There was a general reduction in land under the plough after the Wars, so it is possible that the Paddock reverted to pasture during the following decade.[44] It was this Paddock which was bisected by Henry Palmer, Surveyor for the South Eastern Railway.

Apart from the Postern Farm there were, in 1838, two others – Postern Park and Upper Postern. All three were occupied by separate tenants. But an analysis of land use suggests that they were working to a masterplan, each specialising so as to complement the others.

Land use at the Postern

	Postern Farm per cent	Postern Park per cent	Upper Postern per cent
arable	17.4	60.0	74.0
meadow	49.2	20.0	7.0
pasture	24.3	–	–
orchard	3.5	19.0	5.0
wood	3.1	–	2.0
hops	2.4	–	11.0

Arable and fruit predominates at Postern Park while Upper Postern specialises in arable and hops. The whole forms a mixed farm with hops and fruit grown in equal quantities.

Summary

One general trend over the century was for each original unit to retain its name, size and nucleus of buildings while being combined with adjacent holdings particularly by the larger owners. Cage, Starvecrow and the riparian meadows were apparently worked as one, although under different tenants, and the same applies to Stair/Winchester, with one owner-occupier, and the three farms at the Postern with three tenants. The Tanyard-Eldridges, however, could expand only slightly, and the Parsonage contracted as James-Eldridge West undertook further aggregation towards the Shipbourne Road.

Another general trend was for the larger farmsteads to become more pretentious. They were either built anew like Yardley, Postern House and the second house at the Tanyard, or refaced like Postern Heath. Formal gardens, driveways and lodges were added amenities. On the other hand some of the smaller dwellings like Rat's Castle, the Old Forge and Sanguins, seem to have deteriorated or been subdivided. Cottages often appeared on the boundaries, either for farm labourers or specialist workers like gamekeepers or bailiffs.

As far as evidence for husbandry goes, continuity is more discernible than innovation. Unfortunately there is no indication of yields or breeds of animals. It would be surprising if both were not improved over the period. But on the whole this remained an area of mixed farms, with some signs that hops were, in places, beginning to play a significantly commercial rôle. During the previous century, as Dr Chalklin found, hops were destined, on many farms, only for domestic consumption.

Dr Chalklin's findings for the period 1650-1750 revealed very similar conditions in farming to those found here.[45] Fields being small meant that copse-shaws shielded them from sun and wind, and therefore kept yields low. The heavy soil required several ploughings and harrowings, and a five or six year period of clover fallow after two or three years' continuous sowings of wheat. Inventories allowed Dr Chalklin to observe that while oxen and horses were kept as draught animals and cows were kept for the home consumption of their products, sheep and young cattle were kept for fattening. In seeking to define agrarian regions in the period 1500-1750, Dr Joan Thirsk says that a medieval interest in dairying had probably given way to stock-fattening and pig-keeping over the low Weald.[46] In our area there would appear to have been no great differences between one farm and another.

Conclusions

Broadly speaking the ownership of the two former demesne lands of the Manor, Cage and Postern passed from absentee gentry families in the seventeenth century, through local gentry, yeomen or professional men in the eighteenth, to their descendants in the nineteenth. These descendants were increasing and aggregating their holdings.

The original owners of our three smaller properties are unknown, and it could be that the units themselves, particularly the Tanyard and Winchester, were but recently developed. But they were held by Townsmen following professions or trades. In the opening years of the nineteenth century difficulties of a financial or familial nature led to sales, and the incoming owners were connected with local tenant-farmers or superior tradesmen.

There have been more examples of upward than of downward mobility. Perhaps this is a distorted picture because of the restricted area being studied, but the advancement of families bearing the names Alchin, Simmons, Mugridge, Eldridge and West, is indisputable. Residences were improved, portions for daughters rose, tenants were able to buy land and town houses, testamentary bequests reached four figures, and sons were given a classical education. This prosperity can be seen particularly in the latter part of the eighteenth century, and with the Martins, the Wests, and the Mugridges, it seems to have continued to the end of our period.

During the French disturbances the financial position of some families was difficult. There were mortgaging problems and some bankruptcy. But family arrangements like the duty of sharing out the estate among large numbers of children, or of fathers helping out the neediest, contributed to decline.

Family circumstances could, on the other hand, advance some sons, particularly those with few or no siblings. The son who could expect to inherit both from his father and from a childless uncle, was in a good position, as was the son who could buy the shares of his brothers. The practice of partible inheritance, which was general among our families, did not result in subdivision of units because family arrangements were often made for one to buy out the others. In any case, all the owners on our sites held several other properties.

The legal and medical professions were always well represented in the Town and several members are to be met among our owners. It has been assumed that the Tonbridge attorneys worked at the heart of the Town's affairs from well before our period; they were accepted as respected professionals. They used land as a form of investment. London merchants may have done the same, and, in the early nineteenth century, apothecaries were following suit.

Holding land meant holding office. Whilst the Wests joined the County Administrators, usually the long established gentry – West senior and junior were JPs each for 20 years – and officers in the Militia, they also played an active part in Parish affairs. But it was the men of the 'middling sort' who served as Overseers and Surveyors.

The same surnames often recur over generations, as the following examples show:

Eldridge	1750 – 1777
Mills	1751 – 1793
Milles	1815 – 1830
Mugridge	1743 – 1830
Simmons	1733 – 1800
Waite	1730 – 1800

Social cohesion was, and still is, a feature of everyday life in the Town, and yet family relationships tended to be confined within narrow social strata. Yeomen attested each other's legal documents, and daughters married men of their father's occupations. There were two exceptions. Amy Eldridge advanced her family's fortunes by marrying a London merchant, and John Groombridge married a knight's daughter.

There is some evidence that relationships between landlords and tenants were good, and there seems to have been, at least in the eighteenth century, a real desire for continuity of tenures. The leases on the Cage were of particularly long duration. But landowners followed their own policies regarding covenants and rents, so that averages are of little value. It was the usual practice to lease out land during our period, although there are examples both from the 1780s and the 1830s when the owner held in hand.

Field size and land use appear to have remained remarkably constant. The formation of a large paddock at the Postern is the only significant change in field pattern. All are mixed farms, with hops and fruit playing a smaller role than would have been expected, but with hops increasing slightly over the period. The growing of cereals, and the fattening of sheep were probably the main activities. Every homestead had its orchard and small hopgarden for home consumption.

A clearly discernible trend is for the larger landowners to aggregate by acquiring extra units of land adjacent to their estates, and yet with complementary soils so that, even with different tenants occupying them, farms could specialise according to soil and aspect, and yet produce varied crops with an overall balance.

In 1840, a visitor repeating Horace Walpole's journey would have faced the same jostling sheep and farmers. Gentry, lawyers, tradesmen and dealers would be discussing similar topics. But the railway was approaching. Numbers of Kentish men of all classes had already given their submissions to the Government Select Committee.[47] The overwhelming feeling was one of welcome for the freight trains that were to speed their perishables to market, or for the passenger services that might allow London workers to take up residence here. Tonbridge was astir.

Sources

Three main collections have been used:

Centre for Kentish Studies, Maidstone: catalogue numbers are prefixed K/ in the notes below.
Tonbridge Reference Library: prefixed T1/
Tonbridge Historical Society: prefixed TU1/

Consulted extensively:Tonbridge Parish Registers (TR24/1/29)

References

1   Toynbee, Mrs Paget (ed.), *Letters of Horace Walpole*, vol. III (Clarendon Press, 1903), p111
2   K/U681P1
3   K/U55T424
4   K/U681P25
5   K/U47/17/T159
6   T1/T9 Bundle II
7   T1/A6 Map Cabinet
8   K/U55M385
9   TU1. Apply to author of this essay, via Tonbridge Historical Society
10 Chambers, J D and Mingay, G E, *The Agricultural Revolution* (1966), p47
11 Daily Telegraph, 5 Feb. 1994
12 Boys, J, *General View of the Agriculture of the County of Kent* (2nd edition, 1805)
13 K/U52T465
14 Woodgate, G W et al, *A History of the Woodgates of Stonewall Park and of Somerhill in Kent* (Wisbech,1910)

15 K/U47/17/T159
16 K/U55/T464
17 K/U55/T462
18 K/U55/T424
19 K/U55/T462
20 TU1/Q8/1
21 K/Q/AB58
22 Hasted, E, *The History and Topographical Survey of the County of Kent*, vol. V (republished, 1974) p272
23 Langford, P, *A Polite Commercial People* (Oxford,1989) p192
24 TU1/T76
25 K/U55/T424
26 Robson, R, *The Attorney in Eighteenth Century England* (C.U.P., 1950) passim
27 TU1/9/1
28 TU1/T66
29 K/U47/17
30 TU1/29 Bundle II
31 Filmer, R, *Kent Town Crafts* (Meresborough Books,1982) p39
32 *Register of Baptisms at the Methodist Chapel, Sevenoaks*, 1815 (Sevenoaks Reference Library)
33 Porter, R, *English Society in the Eighteenth Century* (Penguin Books, reprinted 1986) p96
34 K/U47/17/T6
35 K/DRb/Pwr.36.26
36 K/P371/11/2
37 Revd G W Woodgate, op. cit.
38 TU12/T4
39 K/U47/17/T117
40 K/U681/T13
41 K/M385/1-8
42 K/CTR 163 A&B, and TU1/E17
43 Brit. Lib. O.S.D. Sh.100,Kent 1799
44 Chambers and Mingay, op. cit., p131
45 Chalklin, C W, 'The Rural Economy of a Kentish Wealden Parish, 1650-1750', *Agricultural History Review*, vol. 10, part 1 (1962)
46 Thirsk, J, *England's Agricultural Regions and Agrarian History 1500-1750* (Macmillan, 1987). For further reading, see the Select Bibliography.
47 South Eastern Railway Bill, (House of Commons Committee, 1836), vol. 36

List of Subscribers

Presentation Copies

Dr Joan Thirsk, CBE
The Mayor of Tonbridge & Malling, Cllr Terry Barton
The Heritage Development Fund of Kent County Council
The Editor and Authors

Subscribers

Of the five hundred copies of this book printed in November 1994, more than three hundred were for advance subscribers, among whom were:

Norman Acaster
Michael Adams
Susan Adams Business Services
Mrs D Allen
Mr & Mrs M Armstrong
M A Baigent
Derick Baker
Mrs Margaret Baldock
Cllr Mrs O C Baldock
Audrey A Barber
John D Barber
Mr Paul Baxter
Kenneth Beach
Lawrence Biddle
Frank G Blundell
Mr R F Bolam
K J H Bonner-Williams
Mr & Mrs C Bristow

Mr & Mrs John E Brooker
Mr R & Mrs L A Broomfield
Carolyn & Ivor Brown
Frank C Brownhill
Mr & Mrs D N Burford
Jonathan Burgess
Mark Burgess
Peter & Yvonne Burgess
Mr & Mrs C F Burns
Paul Buss
Mr & Mrs F W G Cazalet
T M Chivers
Dr R Clark
Mr & Mrs D L Cosham
Marie Cross
The Crouchers
Chris & Joy Croucher
David Croucher

Anne Curling
Mrs B D'Alton
Christine M Davis
Miss J M Debney
Thelma Dillistone
Mrs Daphne J Duke
Keith Durkin
Jean Durrant
Mr & Mrs H G Edwards
Mr J G Ellis MA
Mrs Doreen Etheridge
A L Evans
Dr & Mrs J M T Ford
Stuart & Jean Forsyth
Georgina Foster
Mrs M Fraser
Maurice P Gilham
M E Going
Anne Goodman
Mr & Mrs R Goodwin
Mr & Mrs D J Green
Mrs Janet Green
Mr & Mrs N D Green
R G Greenhill
Mr & Mrs A Gunton
Mr M J & Mrs L J Guttman-Kenney
J R Haffenden
Mr & Mrs Robert A Hales
Gillian Hankey
Mrs C Hanlay
David & Diana Hardy
Martin & Kate Hardy
Paul & Corinne Hardy
Stella Hardy
Mr & Mrs Tony Hardy
Mrs Barbara Hawkins
Maggie Hawthorn
Mr & Mrs R J Hedley-Jones
Miss Diana Hemeon

Mr & Mrs P L Hemeon
Miss Sally Hemeon
Mr & Mrs K B Hemsley
K Hider
Rev Derek G Hills
Mrs Brenda Hook
Mr & Mrs H D Hook
Mr & Mrs Douglas Hughes
Diana Ivins
Maureen Jackson
Mrs W Jenner
Mrs R O Jermyn
Hazel Johnson
Mr & Mrs David Kemp
Mrs Susan King
Mr R S Larkin
Mr & Mrs S J Larkin
Dr & Mrs O C Legg
Mr & Mrs K H McLaren
Philip & Anne Mallett
Mr & Mrs D Randall Martin
Jack Martin
David Marwood
Bernard & Gwen Michelmore
Mr & Mrs S J W Miller
Roger Millman
Miss B C Mitchener
Jack & Linda Moore
Kenneth Moore
Mr & Mrs Geoffrey E Mortley
Mrs P M Mortlock
Mrs Sandra Mulcahy
Mrs O Mullins
Mr & Mrs Graham Mungeam
Mr Tim Mungeam
Mr Keith Nicholson
Jack K Nutley
Mrs Mary Page
William Parkin

Derek Payne
David Penny
Ann Philp
Dennis & Margaret Pidgeon
Marion Pointer
Mr & Mrs D Postlethwaite
Davyd Power
Margaret Race
Lady Rampton
Mr & Mrs M Rhodes
Marjorie Riley
Linda & Paul Ripley
Gaynor Roberts
Mr & Mrs D M Robins
Mr & Mrs P A Rowe
Mr & Mrs S H Ruck
M F Sawyer
Jayne Semple
Mrs Lily Sheppard
Russell Sherwen
Mr & Mrs J R Shirtcliff
Mr & Mrs C J Shoebridge
Ernest A Sillwood
Joan Simmons
John Simmons
Michael D Simmons
Dr Robert Simmons
Tom Simmons
Ted & Phyllis Skeates

Don Skinner
Mr & Mrs G Smethurst
Mr & Mrs K C Smithers
Mr & Mrs J D Small
Mgr Michael Smith
Peter Swan
Mr & Mrs M Temple
Mr & Mrs D H Tennant
Graeme & Clare Thompson
Tonbridge Castle T I C
Tonbridge Grammar School
    for Girls
Tonbridge Library
Tonbridge Shool
Miss G M Tranter
Mr A F Tullett
D Turley
Mrs E R Ware
William A Warner
A Philip Waterhouse
Vera & Barry Weston
Mr & Mrs Bernard Wheeler
Mrs Margaret Wilkinson
Dr & Mrs A W Wilson
Miss M Woodrow
Gerald Woods
David & Susan Wright
Mr & Mrs G Wright
George & Annie Young